INVENTING
SANTA
CLAUS

The Mystery of Who Really Wrote the Most
Celebrated Yuletide Poem of All-time
"The Night Before Christmas"

BY CARLO DEVITO

CIDER MILL
PRESS

BOOK
PUBLISHERS
KENNEBUNKPORT, MAINE

13-Digit ISBN: 978-1604337358
10-Digit ISBN: 1604337354
This book may be ordered by mail from the publisher. Please include $5.99 for postage and
handling. Please support your local bookseller first!

Books published by Cider Mill Press Book Publishers are available at special discounts for bulk
purchases in the United States by corporations, institutions, and other organizations. For more
information, please contact the publisher.
Cider Mill Press Book Publishers
"Where good books are ready for press"
PO Box 454
12 Spring Street
Kennebunkport, Maine 04046
Visit us on the Web! www.cidermillpress.com

Cover design by Cindy Butler
Interior design by Annalisa Sheldahl
Typography: Goudy Old Style, Nexa Rust Slab, Gotham
Photo Credits, please see pages 190-191

Printed in the United States
1 2 3 4 5 6 7 8 9 0
First Edition

This book is dedicated to my grown sons, Dylan Carles DeVito and Dawson Cordell DeVito. And to my sisters Leigh Ann DeVito Dey and Claudia DeVito Pazmany, and to their children Cary, Vivian, and Madysen.

"When, what to my wondering eyes should appear,
But a miniature sleigh, and eight tiny rein-deer,
With a little old driver, so lively and quick,
I knew in a moment it must be St. Nick."

— "The Night Before Christmas"

Contents

Introduction

Catherine Barnes is a name that probably means nothing to you. To be honest, it meant nothing to me until recently. She was a children's book illustrator who worked on dozens of books, only one of which was important to me.

Catherine B. Sullivan (née Barnes) was a gifted illustrator and artist. According to her obituary she was a "stylish and stunning woman" whose "remarkable creative talents transcended the art world. As an illustrator of children's books and religious items, Catherine was employed with both Hallmark and American Greetings, and enjoyed artistic competition with such notables as Winston Churchill." She illustrated many books, including *The Night Before Christmas, Tip Top Tales, Cinderella, Let's Pretend, A Visit to the New York World's Fair, The Runaway Flea Circus, Jack and the Beanstalk, Pom Pom The Fuzzy Dog, Fairy Tale Favorites, Famous Fairy Tales, Rose in Bloom,* as well as many more for Whitman Publications and others. "Life for Catherine was never limited, as evidenced by her love of family, her faith, and devotion to parish," her notice continued. "She was born in 1918 and passed away at age 90, in 2009, in Washington Township, New Jersey".

It was not until I was researching this book, that by accident, I stumbled upon some illustrations from the book online, and was immediately teleported back in time. Suddenly I saw my childhood room, and the rituals and smells and memories of the time and people came rushing back.

Catherine Barnes came into our family's lives by way of her illustrated Christmas book around 1970 or 1971. We were living in Southport, Connecticut, not far from the old Pepperidge Farm day-old bread store on Route 1. We were near the village downtown area, near Switzer's Pharmacy, the Fairfield Women's Exchange, and the Pequot School (our grammar school), all of which were right next to the charming little New England harbor chockablock with sailboats of all stripes and sizes.

It was while we were living there in this idyllic New England seacoast town that my mother brought home our first encounter with *The Night Before Christmas*. The book had colorful, magical illustrations (Catherine's), depicting a fun, technicolor old Victorian house complete with sleeping dog and cat. There were children with sugarplums snuggled all nice in their beds. And all the rest. In short, it was magical.

During the Christmas season, my mother would read it to us every night. And my little sister and I listened intently.

My little sister, a few years younger than I (although she lies about it now, and tells people that she's *much* younger than I am), was a tiny little thing, with small tiny teeth that eventually required braces, and big brown eyes, with long wavy hair usually done in a ponytail. She was skinny and gangly.

I was no better. I was thin and awkward, with blue eyes, and a big, bushy head of hair (it was the 70s, you have to remember) that resembled a large, dark brown Chia Pet. Poking up out of this tangle of hair stuck a cowlick that made me look like a 70s Alfalfa from the *Our Gang* films. This look was complemented with giant wire-rimmed glasses (because I was already somewhat blind at an early age), and my already screwed-up appearance was capped off by a big gap between my two front teeth.

We were quite the pair.

The particular edition of *The Night Before Christmas* that we listened to so raptly was published by Whitman Publishing in

Racine, Wisconsin. And we loved it. I am not sure if we liked the fact that our mother read it to us, or if we were in love with its stylized art. But we were hooked.

My mother would hold the book hostage, claiming that if we didn't get ready for bed, wash our faces, brush our teeth, and get under the covers, we would not get to hear the story. I locked myself in the bathroom and ran the water, wet the toothbrush, and pretended to do these things, and then walked out exactly the same as before I walked in. Of course, my sister performed these duties admirably.

Catherine Barnes edition

At the time, we lived in a small condominium, with a distant view from our deck of the Atlantic Ocean. My parents were in their late 20s, it strikes me now. Christmas was a magical time. We went to the Christmas bazaar at the Southport Volunteer Fire Company, where my mother had silhouettes cut out, and we colored in paper ornaments with crayons, and bought hand-made felt ornaments that my sister and I picked out.

We had a cathedral ceiling in the living room, and my parents always bought very, very tall trees. My parents went to the same tree farm for many years, run by an old Italian man with a heavy accent who always insisted that my parents take a swig of his homemade wine. "Terrible stuff," my father would say later, making a face. But they always toasted the season with him in good cheer. It was an adventure to see them angle and wiggle and force the tree up the narrow, zig-zag stairs. One year, the tree was too big, and the boyfriend of the retired neighbors' daughter, a West Point cadet, helped my father saw off the bottom two feet of the tree right there in the hallway to get the tree to fit through the doorway.

My sister and I shared a room at that time, I being in second grade and my sister in nursery school. Painted in the color scheme of the period, we had one wall that was a solid olive green. The daybed I slept in had an orange corduroy cover and matching bolsters against the wall. My sister slept in the trundle bed that hid underneath it during the day, and that we pulled out as part of our sleeping routine.

Only once we were under the layers of colorful sheets and thick, blue, woolen blankets would my mother pull out the big, red, oversized children's book, and begin reading. We would interrupt all the time, asking questions about the story, about Santa, about our presents. We constantly pulled and pawed and grabbed and rudely tugged at the book in order to stare at the pictures just a little longer. The colorful spreads were like candy to our eyes. My sister and I seemed particularly preoccupied with the amount and number and kinds of toys Santa

Claus might bring. Some days my mother had the patience for such interrogations, some days she did not.

At the end of the poem, familiar now as we were with it, when it came time to recite the last line, my sister and I would join in unison. "Merry Christmas to all! And to all a good night!"

We would continue asking questions, attempting to find out more about Christmas as well as trying to stave off my mother turning out the light and having to face sleep. Anything to put off actually going to bed!

After my mother had said good night and shut the door, admonishing us (I am sure sometimes, pleading with us) to go to sleep, we each would lie there, under our own covers, and talk.

My sister wanted a Mrs. Beasley doll and crayons, and I wanted Hot Wheels and Major Matt Mason astronaut action figures, or the accompanying Moon Walkers or Moon Space Station. I wanted to collect them all! Then we would talk about any number of things. Family. Friends. Toys. Anything at all to not go to sleep. Sometimes these talks went on for a long time, in the dark, the two of us staring at the ceiling or out the window below our bed into the starry night. It always ended the same, though. I would ask a question or say something, and eventually there would be no response. My sister had made the foul decision to actually fall sleep. Thus abandoned, I too would begin to lose the struggle, fighting all the way, but eventually succumbing myself to that same dormant state.

As with all siblings, my sister and I fought often. As my mother used to say, "It got to the point where I bought every-thing the same: two red balloons, two chocolate ice cream cones, two cherry lollipops, and you still found something to fight over anyway." We made faces, called each other names, and worse. I wish I could tell you it was always her fault, but you and I both know better.

There were a few times we were able to get on, like the time we slept in the hall, attempting to catch Santa Claus, crouched on our knees, sure that this time we would get a glimpse of him. We eventually both failed in our mission, falling asleep in a pile in the hall.

Christmas was always a whirlwind. Presents. Breakfast. Church. Visiting or hosting family, aunts, uncles, cousins. Eventually we moved, and each of us got our own rooms, hap-py, finally, to be rid of one another. Storytime went by the by and the teenage years approached. Christmas lost none of its sizzle, though its appeal began to change. Hanging out with our friends, going off to parties, wanting clothes and money instead of toys and gifts. But our love of the season never diminished. And between the two of us, one of us always had the Catherine Barnes illustrated edition of *The Night Before Christmas* to refer to at least once during the holiday season.

At one point, my mother took the book and put it away

for safekeeping. She returned it to me when I was much older. I had children of my own by then, and it was my turn to read aloud what seemed now like one of the sacred scriptures of the season. The book was now worn and torn and beaten up thoroughly. And so I brought home a new edition to begin the tradition over with. I read it aloud at bedtime, and read it again on Christmas Eve or Christmas night.

Sometimes my boys were good, and sometimes not. But they knew the poem and could recite the last line without fail. And thus becomes an American tradition that has been carried on through countless generations, across two centuries, by thousands and thousands of families across North America and around the world.

"Happy Christmas to all! And to all a good night!"

Myself and my sister Claudia on Santa's lap in 1967

CHAPTER 1

The Troy Sentinel, 1823

It is altogether fitting that this story began at the *Troy Sentinel*. Published by Norman Tuttle at 225 River Street in what is now Troy's historic downtown, it served a readership that lived in Rensselaer County in upstate New York as well as surrounding environs. The semiweekly sheets published therein were the standard-bearer for the metropolitan area from the years between 1823 and 1832. Orville L. Holley served as the newspaper's editor for most of those years, being absent for most of 1826 and 1827.

The region was originally inhabited by the Mahican

Indian tribe. In the mid-1600s, Dutch colonists began arriving, renaming it *Pafraets Dael* (a nod to the patroon Kiliaen van Rensselaer's mother, after whom it was named). In 1664, New York passed from the Dutch to English rule. Derick Vanderheyden established an estate nearby in 1707, and by 1771 it had been laid out in a city grid. The area

Offices of the Troy Sentinel *on River St, Troy, NY which still stand today*

was renamed Troy in 1789 (in a nod to the famous city in Homer's *Iliad*), and incorporated in 1791.

During the War of 1812, Stephen Van Rensselaer of Troy marshaled the New York militia and regular army forces, and Troy was the base of operations wherein quartermaster supplies were shipped in and out. Samuel Wilson, a local butcher and meat packer, was fortunate to supply the military campaign. The apocryphal legend has it that the meat, packed in barrels, was stamped "U.S.," and the soldiers joked that the initials stood for Uncle Sam. Spinmasters in Troy have since claimed the small town to be the point of origin of "Uncle Sam" as a way of describing the U.S. Through Wilson and others supplying the army, by 1816 Troy had become a city. In later years, it would host two professional baseball teams and become a huge steel town (which used the Erie Canal to ship vast quantities west, manufactured via the then-new Bessemer process). Later, shirt and other textile manufacturing gained head way, and the town became known as the "Collar City."

"The pages of the Sentinel," wrote the journalist Ian Benjamin of those early years in the 1800s, "give a glimpse into a bygone era, when commerce was plied almost exclusively on the nation's waterways. Of common occurrence are shipping announcements declaring what goods, such as fabrics or furniture, had arrived and from where, as well as accounts from the building of the Erie Canal, and a series of articles following Marquis de Lafayette on his tour of America. Unlike modern day newspapers, The Sentinel also contained poetry."

The newspaper ran a dedicated poetry column. "Of special note was a poem that appeared in the pages of the December 23, 1823 issue," wrote Benjamin. "It was titled 'An Account of a Visit from St. Nicholas.' While a poetry column ran on page two of each issue, 'A Visit from St. Nicholas' and its preface were not printed within that column's height, next to 'Solomon's Song' and 'Beauty.' Instead, the poem... was sequestered between a marriage announcement and a piece on how to take honey from a hive."

A note from the editor preceded the poem. It read: "We

THE TROY SENTINEL.

TUESDAY, DECEMBER 23, 1823.

For the Sentinel.

ACCOUNT OF A VISIT FROM ST. NICHOLAS.

'Twas the night before Christmas, when all thro'
   the house,
Not a creature was stirring, not even a mouse;
The stockings were hung by the chimney with
   care,
In hopes that St. Nicholas soon would be there:
The children were nestled all snug in their beds,
While visions of sugar plums danc'd in their
   heads,
And Mama in her 'kerchief, and I in my cap,
Had just settled our brains for a long winter's
   nap—
When out on the lawn there arose such a clatter,
I sprang from the bed to see what was the mat-
Away to the window I flew like a flash,   [ter,
Tore open the shutters, and threw up the sash.
The moon on the breast of the new fallen snow,
Gave the lustre of mid-day to objects below;
And then in a twinkling, I heard on the roof
The prancing and pawing of each little hoof.
As I drew in my head, and was turning around,
Down the chimney St. Nicholas came with a
   bound:
He was dress'd all in fur, from his head to his
   foot,
And his clothes were all tarnish'd with ashes and
   soot;
A bundle of toys was flung on his back,
And he look'd like a peddler just opening his
   pack:
His eyes—how they twinkled! his dimples how
   merry,
His cheeks were like roses, his nose like a cherry;
His droll little mouth was drawn up like a bow,
And the beard of his chin was as white as the
   snow;
The stump of a pipe he held tight in his teeth,
And the smoke it encircled his head like a wreath.
He had a broad face, and a little round belly
That shook when he laugh'd, like a bowl full of
   jelly:
He was chubby and plump, a right jolly old elf,
And I laugh'd when I saw him in spite of myself;
A wink of his eye and a twist of his head
Soon gave me to know I had nothing to dread.

The original publishing of A Visit From St.
Nicholas *from the* Troy Sentinel *1823*

know not to whom we are indebted for the following description of that unwearied patron of children — that homely, but delighted personification of parental kindness — Sante Claus, his costume and his equipage, as he goes about visiting the fire-sides of this happy land, laden with Christmas bounties, but, from whomsoever it may have come, we give thanks for it."

ACCOUNT OF A VISIT FROM ST. NICHOLAS.

'Twas the night before Christmas, when all thro' the house,
Not a creature was stirring, not even a mouse;
The stockings were hung by the chimney with care,
In hopes that St. Nicholas soon would be there;
The children were nestled all snug in their beds,
While visions of sugar plums danc'd in their heads,
And Mama in her 'kerchief, and I in my cap,
Had just settled our brains for a long winter's nap
When out on the lawn there arose such a clatter,
I sprung from the bed to see what was the matter.
Away to the window I flew like a flash,
Tore open the shutters, and threw up the sash.
The moon on the breast of the new fallen snow,
Gave the lustre of mid-day to objects below;
When, what to my wondering eyes should appear,
But a miniature sleigh, and eight tiny rein-deer,

With a little old driver, so lively and quick,
I knew in a moment it must be St. Nick.
More rapid than eagles his coursers they came,
And he whistled, and shouted, and call'd them by name:
"Now! Dasher, now! Dancer, now! Prancer, and Vixen,
"On! Comet, on! Cupid, on! Dunder and Blixem;
"To the top of the porch! to the top of the wall!
"Now dash away! dash away! dash away all!"
As dry leaves before the wild hurricane fly,
When they meet with an obstacle, mount to the sky;
So up to the house-top the coursers they flew,
With the sleigh full of Toys and St. Nicholas too:
And then in a twinkling, I heard on the roof
The prancing and pawing of each little hoof.
As I drew in my head, and was turning around,
Down the chimney St. Nicholas came with a bound:
He was dress'd all in fur, from his head to his foot,
And his clothes were all tarnish'd with ashes and soot;
A bundle of toys was flung on his back,
And he look'd like a peddler just opening his pack:
His eyes how they twinkled! his dimples how merry,
His cheeks were like roses, his nose like a cherry;
His droll little mouth was drawn up like a bow,
And the beard of his chin was as white as the snow;
The stump of a pipe he held tight in his teeth,

And the smoke it encircled his head like a wreath.
He had a broad face, and a little round belly
That shook when he laugh'd, like a bowl full of jelly:
He was chubby and plump, a right jolly old elf,
And I laugh'd when I saw him in spite of myself;
A wink of his eye and a twist of his head
Soon gave me to know I had nothing to dread.
He spoke not a word, but went straight to his work,
And fill'd all the stockings; then turn'd with a jirk,
And laying his finger aside of his nose
And giving a nod, up the chimney he rose.
He sprung to his sleigh, to his team gave a whistle,
And away they all flew, like the down of a thistle:
But I heard him exclaim, ere he drove out of sight,
Happy Christmas to all, and to all a good night.

The poem became one of the most reprinted pieces of verse ever produced by an American man or woman of letters. It has become known worldwide. And its vision of St. Nicholas set the tone for the character known as Santa Claus for nearly two centuries.

This is all true. Every scholar will agree that these are the facts of this story.

But who wrote it? That has been one of the great literary mysteries for almost 200 years.

CHAPTER 2

Washington Irving, The Man Who Popularized the American Sinterklass

The American Santa Claus we know today is almost wholly an invention of the Hudson Valley. Indeed, one can honestly say that the fat, jolly old elf we know and love was born in the Hudson Valley.

He came from the great American melting pot, a stew of ethnic stories and stereotypes, simmering with Dutch and English resentment and cohabitation of more than a half century, which was whipped into a big white meringue confection, and served up to American readers in the early- to mid-19th century.

"We think of St. Nicholas—or more commonly, Santa Claus—as a jolly gift-giver donning a red suit and a full, white beard. But did you know that many of our ideas of Santa Claus and the celebration of Christmas were hand-crafted in New York's Hudson Valley?" wrote regional and Christmas historian Karl Felsen. "Dutch settlers, New York City Loyalist newspaper editor James Rivington; John Pintard, one of the founders of the New York Historical Society...the likely writer of 'The Night Before Christmas'; and the American author Washington Irving—together, they were responsible for helping turn a saint into Santa."

Nicholas of Myra (St. Nicholas) was born on March 15, 270 at Patara, Lycia, in Asia Minor and was a historic fourth-century Christian saint and Greek bishop of Myra, also in Asia Minor (what is present-day Demre, Turkey).

As a young man, he made a pilgrimage to Egypt and the Palestine area. Nicholas spent time in a Roman prison as part of the persecutions of Emperor Diocletian. With the ascension of Constantine and that emperor's recognition of the Christian community, Nicholas, like many others, was released. He was counted among those who were there at the Council of Nicaea, a gathering of Christian bishops that Constantine convened. Nicholas died on December 6, 343. More than 700 years later, in 1087, Italian merchants transported his remains and buried him in Bari, Italy.

Over the course of centuries, Nicholas was appropriated by many of the major Christian sects and religions. His rumored habit of secret gift-giving and his forgiving nature made him the patron saint of sailors, merchants, archers, penitent thieves, children, brewers, pawnbrokers, and students around the world. Of course, his most treasured reputation was for his generosity. In the Hudson Valley, his feast day was well regarded by the original Dutch settlers, with whom he eventually came to be known as *Sinterklaas*. Thus St. Nicholas, a real saint, slowly became known as Sinterklaas. He would soon morph into a fictional character, and his name would undergo even further corruption. But how did it happen?

"It was the work of a small group of antiquarian minded New York gentlemen — men who knew one another and were members of a distinct social set. Collectively, these men became known as the Knickerbockers," wrote the historian Stephen Nissenbaum. "The Knickerbocker set inhabited a special niche

Washington Irving

in the world of early-nineteenth-century New York. As a rule its members were of British, not Dutch, descent. They belonged to the Episcopal Church, and more particularly, to its ritually inclined High Church faction. They were part of the wealthy old aristocracy of the city (or at least they identified with it)."

Nissenbaum later wrote, "Like Clement Moore, the knickerbockers who brought St. Nicholas to New York were a deeply conservative group who loathed the democrats and

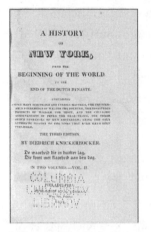

A History of New York *title page*

the capitalists who were taking over their city and their nation. Washington Irving disdainfully summarized in the Knickerbocker History an episode which clearly represented to his readers the Jeffersonian Revolution of 1800: '[J]ust about this time the mob, since called the sovereign people... exhibited a strange desire of governing itself.'"

Though it was eventually Irving who began the popularization of Santa Claus, Felsen asks the question: "[A]re these early iterations the origin of the term Santa Claus — or did they come earlier? A December 23, 1773 post in James Rivington's *New York Gazetteer* described the following: 'Last Monday the anniversary of St. Nicholas, otherwise called St. a Claus, was celebrated at Protestant Hall, at Mr. Waldron's, where a great number of the Sons of that ancient Saint celebrated the day with great joy and festivity.

"What is 'St. a Claus'? Some have guessed a typo, but more than likely, it is a clumsy attempt at the Dutch 'Sinterklaas.' (Dutch continued to be spoken in the Hudson Valley well into the 1800s.) An Englishman, Rivington tried to approximate Sinterklass, and the puzzling 'a' is merely a short vowel that not only mimics the common pronunciation, but also implies that the word isn't English," continues Felsen.

Felsen also points out that John Pintard of the New York Historical Society unwittingly moved St. Nicholas' feast day, which was traditionally strictly observed on December 6 (especially in the time of Jane Austen, for example), and muddied the water in Gotham. For more than a decade, Pintard noted St. Nicholas Day as December 6. But by 1820, he was indicating that "Sancte Claus's" observance was now December 31. "And indeed, there was a custom, as Irving noted, of visiting friends and consuming St. Nicholas cookies on New Year's Day," wrote Felsen. By 1828, Pintard, a great champion of the saint in New York City, was observing St. Nicholas' feast day on December 25. And there it stayed.

The real turning point came with Washington Irving.

Washington Irving was among the most famous American writers at the turn of the century in the early 1800s. He was internationally known, well-traveled, and well-loved abroad as well.

Irving was of Scottish ancestry, the youngest child of

William Irving Sr., from Quholm, Shapinsay, Orkney, and Sarah (née Sanders). The two had wed in 1761. Sarah bore 11 children, only eight of whom survived into adulthood. Washington was born April 3, 1783 at 131 William Street in New York City. He was born the same week when the news came that the Americans had won their self-proclaimed independence. His mother was so thrilled, she named her newborn after the victorious American general. At the age of six, the fledgling author met his namesake, who was serving as the country's president in the temporary capital of New York City.

Irving was a distracted student, who by age 14 was regularly truant from school, much happier to attend local theater or seek adventure elsewhere. In 1789, the same year he met the president, his parents sent him northward out of harm's way during a yellow fever epidemic. He first went to Tarrytown to stay with a friend in the country (where he became acquainted with the town of Sleepy Hollow), and then traveled farther north. It was there that Irving fell in love with numerous old Dutch stories and customs. His travels through the Catskills would provide the setting for the short story "Rip Van Winkle."

"[O]f all the scenery of the Hudson," Irving later wrote, "the Kaatskill Mountains had the most witching effect on my boyish imagination."

After taking a tour of Europe and studying law, Irving passed the bar in New York in 1806. Bored with the law, he and several friends founded a literary magazine named *Salmagundi*. The magazine gained in popularity, and indeed, in its seventeenth issue, dated November 11, 1807, Irving nicknamed New York City "Gotham" (meaning Goat's Town), and the name stuck.

"It's believed that he was inspired by a folk tale called 'The Wise Men of Gotham,'" wrote the journalist Stacy Conradt about why Irving chose that name. "In it, residents of England's Gotham village catch wind that King John will be traveling through their town. Knowing that the king's visit would bring chaos and turn their quiet village into a circus, the citizens of Gotham decided to feign madness—believed to be contagious at the time—to encourage the king to find another path. They put their plan into action by performing crazy stunts, including trying to drown an eel in a pond and building a fence around a bush to prevent a cuckoo from escaping. The shenanigans worked in this story—King John bypassed Gotham in favor of a town with more sense."

In 1809 Irving published his first book under the pseudonym of Diedrich Knickerbocker: *A History of New-York from the Beginning of the World to the End of the Dutch Dynasty*. It was Irving who coined the use of the term Knickerbocker.

In Chapter V, Irving ascribes a dream to his fictional

character, an old Dutchman, Oloffe Van Kortlandt, writing:

> *The worthy Van Kortlandt, in the council in question, urged the policy of emerging from the swamps of Communipaw and seeking some more eligible site for the seat of empire. Such, he said, was the advice of the good St. Nicholas, who had appeared to him in a dream the night before, and whom he had known by his broad hat, his long pipe...*

> **   *   **

> *—and, lo! the good St. Nicholas came riding over the tops of the trees, in that self-same wagon wherein he brings his yearly presents to children. And he descended hard by where the heroes of Communipaw had made their late repast. And he lit his pipe by the fire, and sat himself down and smoked; and as he smoked the smoke from his pipe ascended into the air, and spread like a cloud overhead. And Oloffe bethought him, and he hastened and climbed up to the top of one of the tallest trees, and saw that the smoke spread over a great extent of country—and as he considered it more attentively he fancied that the great volume of smoke assumed a variety of marvelous forms, where in dim obscurity he saw shadowed out palaces and domes and lofty spires, all of which lasted but a moment, and then faded away, until the whole rolled off, and nothing but the green woods were left. And when St. Nicholas had smoked his pipe he twisted it in his hatband, and laying*

his finger beside his nose, gave the astonished Van Kortlandt a very significant look, then mounting his wagon, he returned over the treetops and disappeared.

*   *   *

At this early period was instituted that pious ceremony, still religiously observed in all our ancient families of the right breed, of hanging up a stocking in the chimney on St. Nicholas Eve; which stocking is always found in the morning miraculously filled; for the good St. Nicholas has ever been a great giver of gifts, particularly to children.

Indeed, Irving mentioned St. Nicholas no less than 25 times in his history of the region. As popular as Irving was, and as ubiquitous as Knickerbocker's *History of New York* became, it would be unimaginable for anyone who was publishing in those days to be unaware of it in Gotham and the Hudson Valley. So popular was the book that Charles Dickens himself became aware of Irving's Christmas writings, which influenced Dickens' love of the season.

The saint from Asia Minor, so popular among the Dutch settlers, was slowly being turned into the character we know today as Santa Claus.

"The Santa Claus who was devised in early-nineteenth-century New York was...a conscious reconstruction of that Dutch ritual—an invented tradition," wrote Nissenbaum.

Felsen observed that "What was likely the first depiction of Santa Claus was found in an eight-page pamphlet called 'The Children's Friend,' dated 1821. Published anonymously in New York City, the pamphlet included an illustration of the following stanza showing 'Sancteclaus.' Or 'Santaclaus' in a sleigh being drawn by a single reindeer.

A Children's Friend *original illustration*

"The Children's Friend: A New-Year's Present to the
Little Ones from Five to Twelve
by Arthur J. Stansbury (1821)

"Old Santeclaus with much delight
His reindeer drives this frosty night.
O'er chimney tops, and tracks of snow,
To bring his yearly gifts to you.

The steady friend of virtuous youth,
The friend of duty, and of truth,
Each Christmas eve he joys to come
Where love and peace have made their home.

Through many houses he has been,
And various beds and stockings seen,
Some, white as snow, and neatly mended,
Others, that seem'd for pigs intended.

Where e'er I found good girls or boys,
That hated quarrels, strife and noise,
Left an apple, or a tart,
Or wooden gun, or painted cart;

To some I gave a pretty doll,
To some a peg-top, or a ball;
No crackers, cannons, squibs, or rockets,
To blow their eyes up, or their pockets.

No drums to stun their Mother's ear,
Nor swords to make their sisters fear;
But pretty books to store their mind
With knowledge of each various kind.

But where I found the children naughty,
In manners rude, in temper haughty,
Thankless to parents, liars, swearers,
Boxers, or cheats, or base tale-bearers,

I left a long, black, birchen rod,
Such as the dread command of God
Directs a Parent's hand to use
When virtue's path his sons refuse."

It remains fairly clear that the character, patterns, ideas, and stories had all been established by others by the time *A Visit from St. Nicholas* was first published in Troy in 1823. While the author, regardless of who it was, could lay claim to the language, the stories, like many major works of the day, were borrowed from time, a literary tradition in that era.

CHAPTER 2

Henry Livingston Jr. and the Livingstons of the Hudson Valley

The Livingston family of the Hudson Valley was among the richest, and by some accounts the richest, families in Colonial America. It has been said that certain branches of the Livingston family worked no job for three or four generations (more than 120 years), but simply managed their family's money and remained part of the leisure class.

Indeed, from the Palladian doorway of his palatial mansion in Clermont, New York, Robert Livingston, "The Chancellor," (one of the five committee members who drafted the Declaration of Independence, and the man who administered the oath of office to George Washington upon being sworn in as the first president of the United States) could look out over the mighty Hudson River, and know that every piece of land he could see with the naked eye, up and down the river's length, on both sides of the water, belonged to him. The Livingstons, at the height of their wealth, owned 1,000,000 acres of the Hudson Valley, massive tracts of land on both sides.

The paternal grandparents of The Chancellor's father, Robert Livingston, "The Judge," were Robert Livingston, "The Elder," (1654–1728) and Alida Schuyler (née van Rens-

Henry Livingston Jr.

selaer) Livingston, daughter of Philip Pieterse Schuyler (1628–1683). She had been widowed when she married The Elder. With her came the van Rensselaer and Schuyler fortunes, complete with huge land holdings, which subsequent generations of Roberts extended even further. The Judge had been a prominent Whig politician, equally involved in politics upstate as well as in New York City. Back in those days, the political power mainly rested in Albany and the valley, due to the vast fortunes that had been made there. Preeminent among them were the Livingstons'.

Today, the remains of the Livingston fortune can be seen in the numerous mansions they left behind, up and down the valley's length. Financier Peter Jenrette of Donaldson, Lufkin & Jenrette owns the old Barrytown mansion in Edgewater. Others include Locusts on the Hudson, Montgomery Place, Clermont, Oak Hill, Forth House, Astor Courts, Staatsburg, Locust Grove, and many more.

Clermont Manor

View of Hudson River
from Clermont Manor

They "had 250 years of access to the very best architecture, the best designers, the best real estate," said Pieter Estersohn, a photographer working on a book about the many Livingston homes.

As is evident of the remaining houses in the valley, the Livingstons lived in the grand manner. One of the best examples of the period is the Clermont mansion, in Clermont, New York, just over the Dutchess County border in Columbia County. The ceilings at Clermont were incredibly high and very ornately decorated. Persian carpets lined the floors, English furniture decorated the rooms. Oil paintings hung on all the walls. Loads of books filled the manicured shelves of the house. Fine crystal. Fine china. Expensive bed linens. Quality clothing. Servants.

Montgomery Place

"Many of these grand homes are still standing, although Livingstons own just a few of them," wrote Candace Taylor in The Wall Street Journal. "While some are museums or institutions, many now serve as country homes for high-profile individuals including photographer Annie Leibovitz; hotelier André Balazs; Rolling Stone founder Jann Wenner; CNN host Fareed Zakaria; writer Andrew Solomon; Marc Jacobs co-founder Robert Duffy, and artist Brice Marden."

The Livingstons of Poughkeepsie (in Dutchess County) were less well-off than their Columbia County cousins to the north, but no one was feeling sorry for them. Dr. Henry Livingston Sr. had been born in Kingston, New York,

in 1714. He married Susanna Storm Conklin in 1742, at
the age of 28, his wife being ten years his junior when the
two eloped. Susanna was the daughter of Captain John Jan
Conklin, a veteran of the Dutchess County Militia during
King George's War (where he participated in the relief of
Fort William Henry), and had helped found the Poughkeepsie Dutch Church. He was elected an elder in 1746 and
made a deacon in 1763. He was of the Conferentie party,
maintaining that all ministers must be ordained in Holland.
The Conklin family Bible was in Dutch.

The Dutch had settled New Amsterdam (now New York
City) in 1524. Albany had been discovered by Henry Hudson in 1609, who claimed it for the United Netherlands,
the sponsor of his expedition. Dutch fur traders settled it
in 1614, with the establishment of Fort Nassau. The town
came to be known as Beverwijck, meaning beaver district
(the name Albany came much later). Albany has a unique
history. It is among the oldest surviving European settle-
ments in America and remains the country's longest contin-
uously chartered city.

For 50 years, Dutch settlers filled the valley between the
two points. But the territory was hard to hold. The French
held sway in Canada, with whom the Dutch often clashed,
while also skirmishing with the English to the south. Then,
in 1664, the English conquered New Amsterdam. Three

years later the Treaty of Breda and the later Treaty of West-
minster confirmed that the Dutch relinquished their colonial rights to New Neatherlands (including Beverwijck and
New Amsterdam) in return for their unchallenged control
of the Island of Run in North Maluku (amazingly rich in
nutmeg spices) and the country of Suriname.

Despite the official name change, New York, as it was
now called, remained firmly Dutch in its heritage and
influence for another half century. Livingstons were all
taught Dutch. In the surviving Livingston homes, many
artifacts, including the Bible and other books, could be
found in Dutch. All remained in contact with the mother
language for many generations. (This tidbit of information
is important to our story.)

Henry Livingston Sr. and his wife, Susanna, settled
at Poughkeepsie, where he had a grant for life. He served
as clerk of Dutchess County from 1742 to 1789, and from
1759 to 1768 as a member of the assembly from that
county as well.

"Henry Livingston (1714–1799) bought a small house at
Poughkeepsie in 1742 and added to it from time to time,
until when he died it had become of generous proportions.
During the nineteenth century it was still further enlarged
and ultimately it was a rambling structure full of the story
of the life of a family for a century and a quarter," wrote the

local historian Helen Wilkinson Reynolds.

The house was an impressive one, known for its forward-thinking conveniences and elegance. It had eight rooms, a pantry, a large kitchen, and servants' quarters (several of the servants were probably slaves). There were vegetable gardens, flower gardens, an orchard of more than 300 peach trees and 600 apple trees, and a stand of 600 locust trees, presumably for timber.

Henry Sr. died on February 10, 1799. His obituary in the *Poughkeepsie Advertiser* read:

Henry Livingston Sr.'s obituary

> *On Sunday last, the 10th inst. at 1 o'clock, P.M. Henry Livingston, Esq. for about sixty years a much respected inhabitant of this place, closed his eyes in death at the advanced*

age of 84 years 5 months and 3 days – he ever maintained a character of punctuality and integrity, filled for the most of his life important offices, with the greatest exactness, ability and public confidence – he was ever a republican in principle – and demonstrated till the last that he was no friend to aristocracy or monarchy. He died rejoicing that the Lord reigns – and some of his last words (about an hour before his death) were "Let all creatures and things rejoice in and praise the Lord."

When his father died, Henry Jr. was prominently featured in his father's will:

I give and bequeath unto my son Henry and to his heirs and assigns forever the one whole equal tenth part of all my estate both real and personal of what kind soever which shall remain after the uses afore mentioned to have and to hold the same unto the said Henry his heirs and assigns forever, subject nevertheless to a deduction of One thousand three hundred and fifty pounds being the valuation of a farm and estate granted to him by a deed of gift which sum (agreeable to the present estimate of gold and silver) it is my will shall be considered as a part of his divident already apportioned to him and that he shall receive no part of my estate as any proportion of the legacy hereby bequeathed until the rest of my children shall each have received a sum equal to the valuation of the estate

given to him and it is my will that he shall be bound to fulfill
the tenor of an obligation entered into by him for that purpose.

In March 1799, the house of Henry Livingston Sr. and the associated 80 acres of lands were put up for sale by the surviving five sons: Gilbert, John, Henry, Robert, and Beekman.

"The executors of the will of Henry Livingston sold this homestead on March 7, 1800 to Henry Alexander Livingston (1776–1849), a grandson of the first owner," Reynolds continued. "The latter died in 1870 and in 1872 the Hudson River Iron Company bought it. The company's successors, the Phoenix Horseshoe Company, used the house as an office-building for many years but in 1910 tore it down. At that time the mantel in the southwest parlor was presented to the Daughters of the American Revolution and set up in the Clinton Museum. A brass grate, once encircled by this mantle, is shown in an old photograph in the Year Book of the Dutchess County Historical Society for 1919." It remains there today.

This was the world Henry Livingston Jr. was born into. Power. Wealth. And a sea of endless familial connections from Albany to New York City.

Henry Livingston Jr. was born on October 13, 1748 in Poughkeepsie. He was a somewhat careless student, los-ing books, constantly flouting the rules of grammar, and ignoring his Latin studies, much to the chagrin of his teachers. One of them was the Reverend Chauncey Graham, a New Englander, who was pastor for some 30 years of the English-speaking Presbyterian congregation at Brinckerhoffville in Dutchess County, and conducted there a school as well. Reverend Graham and Henry Sr. were both learned men, and it is apparent from correspondence that they shared volumes of books with one another, and recognized in each other a companion in literature. In May of 1753, for example, Graham thanked Henry Sr. for the lending of a library of tragedies.

At the age of 22, Henry Jr. fell in love with a young woman named Sarah Welles. Henry called her by the nickname Sally. At the time, Sarah was still living at home with her parents, Reverend Noah Welles and Abigail Woolsey (the daughter of Reverend Benjamin Woolsey and Abigail Taylor). Reverend Welles graduated Yale in 1741 (where he served as a tutor for a year shortly after that) and served 30 years as a minister in Stamford, Connecticut. Welles "was also known for his association with William Livingston in the defense of Presbyterianism against Anglican attacks. Welles' imagination was vivid and poetical, his intellect vigorous, and his learning extensive. His manners at the same time were an unusually happy compound of politeness and dignity. In his conversation he was alternatively sprightly and grave as occasion dictated, and entertaining and instructive. At the same time he was an excellent minister of the Gospel, exemplary in all the virtues of the Christian life, an able preacher, a wise ruler of the church, and an eminently discreet manager of its important concerns," reported one magazine of the day.

"While Henry's brothers chose careers in the law and in the Dutch Reformed Church, Henry's path lay on the land he had known from his birth, the estate on the Hudson River that had belonged to his father, Henry Sr., and before that, to his grandfather, Captain John Conklin. In 1771, at the age of twenty-three, Henry became the owner of Locust Grove, the southern most part of his father's land. Rath-

Locust Grove

er than building right on the River, Henry built on the Post Road, our Route 9, and the place where his home was can still be seen at Locust Grove today," wrote Mary S. Van Deusen, a distant relative.

From the original patent of land running from Poughkeepsie south to the town of Clinton, to the one hundred acres of land making up present-day Locust Grove, Locust

Grove has had a rich history. It has been speculation land, a working farm, the land of a gentleman farmer, a country estate, and, now, an historical site.

THE OLD LIVINGSTONE MANSION.

Old Livingston Mansion

Henry was a romantic. "To discover Henry is to throw out all your notions of 18th-early 19th century life in small town America. Henry was not living on the primitive frontier, nor was he absorbed in the question of survival to the exclusion of all else. Henry's table was set with silver, and he was as concerned with art and poetry, literature and music, as anyone whose ancestors were getting their masters' degrees back in the 1400's. Blessed with the open-minded New York Dutch heritage, Henry's views on the education of women, reverence for nature, and respect for Native Americans are views we can easily appreciate today," continued Van Deusen.

At the age of 25, Henry wrote to Sarah:

Henry Livingston Sr.'s house

New York, December 30th, '73

A happy Christmas to my dear Sally Welles.

Next Tuesday evening I hope to see the Girl for whom alone I would well bear to live. Yes, my dear creature, next Tuesday evening, if my God spares my life, I hope to tell you I am as sincerely your friend, as constantly your admirer & as religiously your lover as when I sat by your side & vow'd everlasting affection to you.

I well know you will call this the lover's Cant. Call it so, my love — call it anything — I know & swear its truth and wrap myself up in my own Integrity.

I this moment parted from our good friend Miss Nabley Bostwick; she told me that she Imagined I was return'd to Poughkeepsie as she had not seen me in 2 or 3 days; I told her I was not return'd to Poughkeepsie.

It's whispered about among our friends here that we are like to lose my Cousin Abbe Lloyd this winter as her acquaintance here have a design upon her and intend to get her here if they can. I hope their machinations may prove in vain, for I esteem my Cousin much.

Miss Bostwick will give you an account of the destruction of our Governor's house in the Fort last night; of the terror of the Inhabitants & the great loss our worthy commander in chief has received.

I see Miss Suky & Sally Billy Livingstons every day. They constantly tell me that you are sensible & are very much your friend; their father is in Town & will write to your good parent. I hope heaven will bless your good parent.

My sisters are dying to see and be acquainted with you; and I dare say ardently hope their brother may be successful in his addresses to the heighth of all.

I wish I had been prudent enough to have procured a good private stable for the horse I shall ride up & keep in Stanford this winter–however, I must look about when I come there. To-morrow I expect to send up my necessarys with Capt. Sellick.

Remember me, my dear Love, to my friends and relations at Stanford; and remember, my Love, that of all your friends, none loves you so sincerely as your

– Harry Livingston

Reverend Noah Welles married Henry and Sally in Stamford, Connecticut, on May 18, 1774. In his lifetime, Henry "held the positions of Major of the 3rd NY, Commissioner of Sequestration, Dutchess County Coroner, Justice of the Peace, Principal Assessor, and commissioner of Bankruptcy," according to Van Deusen.

The average year, and average day, before the Revolution saw Henry living like any other wealthy and prosperous land-owner of the time. He engaged several Irish immigrants as

New york Decemr. 30th/73

A happy Christmas to my dear Sally Welles

Next tuesday evening I hope to
see the Girl for whom alone I could will live to live
— Yes my dear creature next tuesday evening if my
God spare my Life I hope to tell you I am as
sincerely your friend, as constantly your admirer &
as religiously your lover as when I sat by your
side & vow'd everlasting affection to you

— I well know you will call this the lovers Cant
— Call it so my love — call it any thing — I
know & swear its truth and wrap myself up in my
own Integrity

I this moment parted from our good
friend Miss Nabby Bostwick; she told me that she
Imagined I was return'd to Poghkeepsie as she had
not seen me in 2 or 3 days, I told her I was not return'd
to Poghkeepsie

We whisperd about among our friends
here that we are like to loo my Cousin Allie Styd this
winter as her acquaintance here have a design upon her
and intend to get her if they can — I hope their
machinations may prove in vain, for I esteem
my Cousin much —

Miss Bostwick will give you an account
of the distruction of our Governors house in the Fort
last night, of the terror of the Inhabitants, & the
great risk our worthy commander in Chief has escaped

I see Miss Suky & Sally Billy Livingston every day.
They constantly tell me that you are sensible & are
very much your friend ; their father is in Town
& will write to your good parent ___ I hope heaven
will bless your good parent ___

My sisters are dying to see and be
acquainted with you : and I dare say ardently
hope their brother may be successfull in his address
to the height of all his hopes ___

I wish I had been prudent enough to have
procured a good private Stable for the horse I shall ride
up & keep at Stanford this winter ___ however I must
look about when I come there ___ Tomorrow I expect to
send up my ____ with Capt Gillet ___

Remember me my dear love to my friends
and relations at Stanford ___ and remember my
love that of all your friends none loves you
so sincerely as your Harry Livingston

Sally Wheeler

(Opposite, and above) Henry Livingston's letter
to Sally. Note the use of "Happy Christmas," a
salutation he used more than once.

farmhands, planted vegetables, fruits, orchards, and groves; and husbanded cows, sheep, pigs, and chickens. He bartered and traded with other local farmers.

In his diary, he recorded everything. He bought bushels of potatoes, buckwheat, sugar loaf, linseed oil, salt, even a dog from a local boat man. He was fond of snuff. He did surveying for any number of local landowners. Henry recorded when he wrote love letters to Sally. He even recorded buying lottery tickets (though he never recorded winning anything).

But by July of 1775, Henry was quickly becoming embroiled in the impending American Revolution. His name was first put on a subscription list (akin today to being drafted) that July, but was erased from those rolls later in the month by John Holt for a price of six shillings. On August 2, his brother Gilbert told Henry that Gilbert had won him a commission as a major over several of their cousins, and that Henry had better take it. It was around this time that Henry and Sally's first child, Catherine, was born.

In mid-August, Henry wrote to Colonel James Clinton, the brother of George Clinton, the future Governor of New York:

Poughkeepsie August 19th 1775

Dr. Sir

I have the pleasure to inform you that yesterday afternoon my wife was a Joyfull mother of a fine daughter — a circumstance in providence I highly rejoice at — You know the feelings of a father Sir on these occasions However I expect to be ready almost or quite as soon as the men here — As no man enters with more zeal into the service of his country than myself — Captain Dubois is now by me & tells me His men are in high spirits & want to be in motion & only want camp kettles & blankets to march immediately — Captain Billings writes to you himself — I must with sorrow tell you the Committees of this county had had but very little success [(?)] in purchasing arms Only the Committee of Poughkeepsie have done well. That precinct alone have furnished between 30 & 40 flintlocks that with little of the gunsmiths aid may do very well — I waited the result of the County Committees proceedings before I proceed [to]take any other method, & wait now for further orders in this particular — The county committees however I am informed this moment are resolved to impress[(?)] arms from these gentlemen that state the liberties of America — perhaps a line from you directing in this affair may be very necessary

If by your influence Sir you can any way get Doctor Cooke with us twould give universal satisfaction — I know the man,

& our family & neighborhood have long experienced the effects
of his skill — & for my part it would considerably alleviate the
evils of a campaign to have a surgeon at hand whose abilities
was well apris'd of & could confide in, My Brother Doctor.
Livingston was with me yesterday & desires his love to you.

   I am sir your humble servant
   Henry Livingston Jun.

By August 25, Livingston was on the move, noting in
his diary, "Embark'd on board Cap't Jacksons sloop at 5
o'clock in the afternoon (who had on board Col'o [James]
Clinton, Mr. Drake sutler & Cap't [John] Nicholson with
his company. We sail'd in company with Cap't [Benjamin]
North, [Anthony] Van Shaack, & [John] Gale each with men
on board. In the evening Van Shaack & Gale got aground
on Esopus meadows." A few days later, he wrote, "August
27. — Our sloop arriv'd at Kingston landing ab't 6 o'clock in
the morning of the 26th. The Coll'o & a few more went on
shore. Breakfasted, got on board & with a fair wind hoisted
anchor at 9 o'clock on our way to Albany, arriv'd at that city
at 5 o'clock in the afternoon."

In early September Henry wrote to Sally, "my dear & I
have already wrote to you more than you will care to peruse
at one sitting: therefore think it best to conclude, especially
as I must be up early....And yet somehow or another I do not

know how to conclude either, when writing to the woman my soul loveth....It's something like a personal taking because we linger & dither and seem to wish to evade sorrowing scenes — & now by the bye I must take notice of a passage in your letter herein you seem to think a little hard of my hurrying away from you too soon when I took my leave of you... God knows how I suffer'd when I left a room which contained my Heaven upon Earth!"

He finished his letter with his earliest recorded poem, his thoughts on his first-born child as he headed off for war:

On my little Catherine sleeping

Sweet Innocent lye still & sleep,
While chearfull seraphs vigils keep,
To ward of ev'ry shaft of death
That may be wing'd to seize thy breath.

Dear Infant how serene you lay,
Nor heed the bustle of the day!
Thy little bosom knows no care,
For guilt neer lay & wrankled there;
In thee all troubles die & cease,
And all is quiet all is peace.
How much unlike thy Father's life

Amid the Din of Arms & strife!
The tumult and the noise of war

Forever thundring in his ear.
Thy mother too has shed her tears
Has heav'd her sigh & known her fears.
Her lips hath not forgot to press
The bitter cup of keen distress.

And Thou sweet Babe will soon perceive
That to be mortal is to greive;
That as the spark will upward fly,
So man still lives to mourn & dye.

By October, Henry and his retinue had joined forces with General Richard Montgomery, an Irish-born immigrant who had attended Trinity College, Dublin and who had served in the British Army, near Fort Ticonderoga. This was to be part of the Invasion of Quebec, the first campaign of the war that the Con-

General Richard Montgomery

tinental Army initiated. The objectives were to take Fort Saint Jean, Montreal, and drive General Carleton from Quebec City as well. It was a tall order.

Fort Ticonderoga had fallen to Ethan Allen and Benedict Arnold in May of 1775. Livingston recorded:

October 11. – A Council of War held at the Generals Tent at which only the Field officers of the army attended. When the General recommended building a Battery west of the forts of St. John But the motion was unanimously opposed by the Officers who were of the opinion as one man, that a Battery erected on the east side of the lake opposite the Forts would make a greater impression on our enemys. On that points being carried the General Ordered Coll'o Clinton and 200 of his men to go upon that Business. The Col'o pitch'd upon myself to go with him, leaving Coll'o [Cornelius D.] Wynkoop with the remainder of our Reg't on the west side of the Lake. Cap't Nicolson, Dubois, Billings & Denton were pitch'd upon to go with us. At 3 o'clock in the afternoon we set off for the east shore in 7 Batteaus and proceeding down to where a road had been just cut on the east side & coming within little more than half a mile of the Fort they gave us several shot with Ball but every one went too high. As we were landing & for some time after we were landed they fired briskly with grape shot from the Fort but by the good providence of God we had not a single man hurt. We made no Regular Encampment but lodged about in the woods as well as we could for this night.

By October 14, Livingston and his group had built a fortified position and created a battery.

> About 1 o'clock The Artillery men arrived from the Grand camp, when we began a heavy fire on the Enemy. Our Batteries on the other side were not Idle also. The Enemy bestow'd their attention chiefly on us, their fire being heavy & well serv'd the beginning of the afternoon but towards evening it slack'd much & we gave them the 2 last shots. They fired shells at us chiefly as their balls could make no impression on our Battery. We lay so near them that they soon learned to throw their shells with great exactness. But altho they were all day continually Bursting over our peoples heads or at their feet, we never lost one man by them, or had even one wounded. Early in the morning The Regulars warp'd their Schooner & ran Galley close up to the North redoubt & full in our view. We shot so many Balls thro her that next morning she lay careen'd so low that the water ran into her port holes.

A small skirmish, a small victory.

Then on November 2, word came that Montgomery's troops had captured Fort St. Jean. After further attacks, Carleton withdrew from Montreal to Quebec City, and Montgomery captured St. Paul's Island with his troops six days later.

While at Three-Mile Point, Livingston sent letters to Montgomery when a small group of British soldiers arrived in two large ships and two sloops coming up the river. Livingston wrote to Montgomery while watching the British make their way up the river to engage Henry and his men. "Our troops are determined and in great spirits....The spirits of the men seem to increase in proportion to the number of the enemy. I cannot but esteem myself fortunate that indisposition prevented me from returning with you, as it has given me an opportunity of being present at a battle in which I promise myself the pleasure of seeing our army flushed with victory."

The British advance was repelled.

On November 13, Montgomery and his troops marched into Montreal, which Carleton had abandoned. He and his staff felt that the defense of the city would be immensely costly and not worth the sacrifice strategically.

Livingston, who arrived the following day, described what he encountered: "The town is not paved: & if it was not for a narrow walk of stones projecting out about 2 feet from the houses the streets would be impassable in the spring & fall—While I was there the mud in the streets was full half leg deep. In Montreal happy is that man who can keep the wall. Fryday is their market day & provision then of almost any kind (fish excepted) is to be had cheap and in great

Benedict Arnold

plenty. The market place has no roof to it—consisting only of a floor & Butchers blocks. It stands in the middle of a square & on market day the street all around is crowded with hucksters of one kind or another—St. Luke La Carnes house (the best in town) fronts the market."

On November 18, Livingston left Montreal to make his way home for the winter. He arrived home on December 22, writing in his diary, "A little after noon I arrived in safety at my house. The God of all mercy be adored for his goodness to an unworthy sinner!"

Livingston was right to be grateful. Montgomery and Arnold had joined forces, and in a final push to destroy what was left of Carleton's army, they attacked Quebec City on December

Death of General Montgomery in the Attack on Quebec December 31, 1775

31. General Carleton, whose forces had seemingly been on the run up to this point, held firm. The attack was disastrous, a severe loss for the Continental Army, and Montgomery was killed.

A year later, Henry was at home, celebrating the birth

of his son on Christmas Day. Tragically, the boy died of a burn shortly after he turned one year old. Henry wrote this moving tribute to his lost infant son:

Henry Livingston Jr.'s poem to his son

To the memory of Henry Welles Livingston
who died of a burn on the 6th day of January 1778
aged 1 year & 13 days

A gentle spirit now above
Once animated what lies here
Till heav'n announc'd in tenderest love
"Ascend Immortal to yon sphere."

The lambkin at the great behest
Gave up its life without one groan.
When lo! in robes supernal drest
He found the bright abodes his own!
Most glorious and delightful scenes

Rush'd full upon his raptur'd sense:
Beyond what fancy ever dreams,
Or Eden knew in innocence.

Adieu! Adieu! my sweet boy,
Adieu till life's vain dream be o'er;
Then with a parent's keenest joy,
I'll cling to Thee to part no more.

On July 31, 1778, a second son was born. Sarah and Henry decided to name him Henry Welles Livingston II.

Five years later, Sarah Welles passed away on September 1, two months shy of her 31st birthday. A devastated Henry wrote:

To the memory of Sarah Livingston
who was born on the 7th of Novr. 1752
& died Sepr. 1st, 1783

BEYOND where billows roll or tempests vex
Is gone the gentlest of the gentle sex!
— Her brittle bark on life's wild ocean tost
Unequal to the conflict soon was lost.
Severe her sufferings! much, alas, she bore,
Then sunk beneath the storm & rose no more.

But when th' Archangel's awful trump shall sound
And vibrate life thro all the deep profound
Her renovated vessel will be seen,
Transcendant floating on the silver stream!
All beauteous to behold! serene she glides
Borne on by mildest & propitious tides;
While fanning zephyrs fill her snow white sails
And aid her passage with the friendliest gales
Till safe within the destin'd port of bliss
She furls her sails and moors in endless peace.

Ten years later, Henry remarried. His new bride was Jane McLean Patterson, 24 years old when she married the 45 year-old Henry. She bore him many children, including Elizabeth Davenport Livingston, Charles Patterson Livingston, Sidney Montgomery Livingston, Edward George Livingston (sometimes known as Edwin), Jane Patterson Livingston, Helen Platt Livingston, and Susan Catherine Livingston.

For the next three decades, Henry remained an important figure in Dutchess County and Hudson Valley life. He chaired the general elections board meetings, was a judge, continued surveying, took part in political discussions, and continued the work of a farm owner. Letters like this one show Henry's involvement and reliance on his children in running their farm while he was away on business:

John Warren's in the Highlands, May 2d. Sunday morn.

Dear Boy:

I rec'd your letter & 3 specs. The letter & 3 specs were all much acceptable.

I am engaged here in a very fatigueing business but I keep my health perfectly & if nothing intervenes materially to interrupt, shall finish the field work, say the 15th instant.

You will see our household, I trust, as often as you conveniently can, & let me hear from you twice during this week. On Saturday perhaps I may come up. Tell our boys, that as it is now herring time, they must frequently look at the woods for fear of fire getting in the leaves, especially as the weather is uncommonly dry at this time.

I take it that James will this week get to plowing. His horses must have grain & hay then, by all means. Mr. Ingraham, I hope, can let us have ½ a load more & 1 or 2 loads of wood. [You] can procure Indian corn in the stores. When you next see dear Mamma, bow down to the very floor & kiss your left hand & press it to your bosom for me, & squeeze and kiss Jane & Edwin heartily for ditto. Shake Sid's and Charley's fists. You have my best affection, my sweet boy.

Henry W. Livingston, Esq.,
Poughkeepsie

Throughout his life, Henry wrote verse and published it in local papers under the initial — R. His personal papers are filled with poems, many elegies (which were a common poetical theme and style of the day), Valentine's Day lines, lines to children, a rebus, an acrostic, birthday wishes, political poems, and even lines about farming. Most interesting for our story, among several rhyming couplets was the following poem:

Translation of a letter
from a tenant of Mrs. Van Kleeck
to that lady, dated Jany 1787

My very good landlady, Mistress Van Kleeck,
(For the tears that o'erwhelm me I scarcely can speak)
I know that I promi'd you hogs two or three
(But who knows his destiny? Certain not me!)
That I promis'd three hogs I don't mean to deny
(I can prove that I had five or six upon sty.)

Three hogs did I say? Three sows I say then
Pon' honour I ne'er had a male upon pen.

Well Madam, the long and the short of the clatter
For mumbling & mincing will not better the matter;

And murder and truth my dear mammy wd say
By some means or other forever saw day;
And Daddy himself, as we chop'd in the wood
Would often observe that lying wan't good.

Tell truth my sweet fellow—no matter who feels it:
It ne'er can do hurt to the man who reveals it.

But stop! —While my Dady and Mammy's the subject
I am running aside the original object —

The sows my sweet madam — the sows I repeat
Which you and your household expected to eat.
Instead of attending their corn and their swill
Gave way to an ugly he-sow's wicked will.

When 'twill end your good lady-ship need not be told
For Nature is still, as she hath been of old;
And when she cries YES, mortals may not cry NO

So Madam farewell, with my holliday bow.

The clatter-and-matter couplet stands out immediately, as well as the sing-song air of the structure. The same rhyming scheme would pop up later in *A Visit from St. Nich-*

olas, in the lines, "When out on the lawn there arose such a clatter, I sprang from my bed to see what was the matter." This is such a unique pairing of words that it would seem like a fingerprint to later literary sleuths. That year, 1787, the poem was published anonymously in the *Country Journal* and *Poughkeepsie Advertiser*. Thus began a fairly long career in publishing poetry publicly, albeit anonymously.

Another poem appeared in the *New York Magazine, or Literary Repository* in February of 1791:

EPITHALAMIUM

'TWAS summer, when softly the zephyrs were blowing,
And Hudson majestic so sweetly was flowing;
The groves rang with music and accents of pleasure,
And nature in rapture beat time to the measure:
When Strephon and Phillis, so true and so loving,
Along the green lawn were seen arm in arm moving;
Sweet daffodils, violets, and roses spontaneous,
Wherever they rambled sprang up instantaneous.

The ascent the lovers at length were seen climbing,
Whose summit is grac'd by the temple of Hymen:
The Genius presiding, no sooner perceiv'd them,
But spreading his pinions, he flew to receive them;

With kindest of greetings pronounced them welcome;
While holliday's clangour rang loud to the welkin.

The obvious connection here is that he has started off the poem with the word "'Twas" and linked it directly to a season, just as the opening line of *A Visit from St. Nicholas* begins, "'Twas the night before Christmas." Another literary fingerprint. "Livingston's verse," wrote the famed literary sleuth MacDonald P. Jackson, "was never gathered into a printed book. He contributed poems anonymously or under pseudonyms...as did many other writers of his time, or addressed them to his children, nephews, nieces, other relatives, and friends. But the survival of bound manuscript leaves in which many of his poems are written out in his own handwriting allows a solid corpus of authentic works to be formed."

According to Mary S. Van Deusen, "A man of deep faith, Henry had a joy of life that came from being raised in a loving and close family. Whether writing from the point of view of a lump of gold still deep in the ground, or an ancient pine tree ruminating on the history it had seen, he could always be relied upon to see the world in a completely different way. A fair king darts through Henry's world in a nutshell drawn by crickets, while a night sprite awaken's him to a New Year's Eve nightmare."

He was still composing poetry at the time of his death in 1828. His extensive family mourned him deeply. Family members told of how their aunt Gertrude Livingston, daughter of Robert R. Livingston, "The Judge," recalled her mother retelling a dream Henry had once told her. He said he was walking in a garden,

Henry Livingston Jr.'s grave

"and that a hoe fell from Heaven. He pickt up the hoe & saw within it these words 'If Henry Livingston will use this hoe diligently he shall live to be 79 years old.'" Henry died at age 79.

Upon his death, there were no notes or papers left behind anywhere to suggest that he had written the famed poem about Christmas known as *A Visit from St. Nicholas*. Nor were there any public acknowledgments linking him to the poem, which had been published six years earlier, or claims by him to be linked to it.

But the story was only just beginning.

CHAPTER 4

Clement C. Moore, The Poet of Chelsea

Eight days before Henry Livingston Jr., Benjamin Moore was born on October 5, 1748 in Newtown, New York (now Elmhurst, Queens) to Samuel Moore and Sarah (née Fish) Moore. Benjamin's great-grandfather had been the first Independent minister in New England, John Moore. Benjamin attended King's College (known today as Columbia University). He graduated in 1768 and three years later earned his master's degree.

With an eye toward following in his grandfather's footsteps, Benjamin traveled to England. Bishop Richard Terrick ordained Benjamin in Fulham Palace on June 24, 1774. A year later, he was named assistant rector at Trinity Church in New York City, located in lower Manhattan. It was a prestigious placement. Four years later he married Charity Clarke, the daughter of British officer Major Thomas Clarke, a veteran of the

Bishop Benjamin Moore

French and Indian War. Clarke was well off and in possession of a very large country estate that came to be known as Chelsea. The Manhattan locale stretched from what is now 19th Street to 24th Street, and from Eighth Ave to the Hudson River. Clarke had named it for the Royal Hospital Chelsea, a retirement home in London for soldiers.

Trinity Church

Charity was 31 when she married Moore in 1778, one year older than her husband. Her father had passed away in 1776, on the eve of the Revolution. Moore had officially remained neutral during the war.

The literary scholar Martin Gardiner maintains that "[d]uring the Revolution he never wavered in his loyalty to England." But the letters of his wife,

Charity, written before their marriage and preserved at Columbia University, show her a critic of the policies of the British monarchy.

According to the Revolutionary War historian Maggie MacLean, "In her early 20s, Charity Clarke was a young New York City woman with strong opinions about the growing tensions caused by Great Britain's tightening grip on the American colonies. Between 1768 and 1774, she wrote a series of letters to her cousin Joseph Jekyll, a London lawyer. These letters show her disdain for the policies of the English Monarchy and her growing sense of patriotism in the period leading up to the American Revolution."

Benjamin Moore house

MacLean continued, "The Townshend Acts of 1767 wanted to strengthen the power of the British parliament, which would simultaneously strengthen the power of royal officials. [Charles Townshend, the Chancellor of the Exchequer] convinced the Parliament to pass a series of laws imposing new taxes on the colonists for lead, paint, paper, glass, and tea imported by colonists."

Charity wrote to Jekyll in London on November 6, 1768,

"When there is the least show of oppression or invading of liberty you may depend on our working ourselves to the utmost of our power."

On March 31, 1769, Clarke again registered her anger and consternation, writing, "The attention of every American is fixed on England. The last accounts from thence are very displeasing to those who wish a good understanding between Britain and her colonies. The Americans are firm in their resolution of no importations from England. The want of money is so great among us that land sells for less than half price. The merchants have no cash to buy bills of exchange, which are now very low."

The following June, Clarke announced her readiness to join "a fighting army of Amazons," who would take to the hills, if necessary, to flee the oppressive British: "If you English folks won't give us the liberty we ask...I will try to gather a number of ladies armed with spinning wheels [along with men] who shall all learn to weave & keep sheep, and will retire beyond the reach of arbitrary power, clothed with the work of our hands, feeding on what the country affords...In short, we will found a new Arcadia."

The last surviving letter of Charity's to Jekyll from before the war is dated September 10, 1774.

On what instance pray are the Americans called Rebels?
What have they done to deserve the name? They have asserted
their rights, and are determined to maintain them. Great Brit-
ain stands ready to destroy her sons for inheriting her spirit.

What care we for your fleets and armies, we are not going
to fight with them unless drove to it by the last necessity, or the
highest provocation....Though this body is not clad with silken
garments, these limbs are armed with strength. The soul is
fortified by Virtue, and the love of Liberty is cherished within
this bosom.

A proud, ambitious Minister [Lord North] governs in Brit-
ain. By his sophistry makes the King deaf to the remonstrances
of his subjects, by his bribery obtains the majority of Parlia-
ment, and by his power would spread tyranny to the western
continent.

But its inhabitants are not sunk in luxury, nor are they
clouded by pomp. Their eyes watch over their liberty, observe
every encroachment and oppose it. And is this their crime in
your eyes, my Cousin? Do you condemn them for not being fool-
ish enough to give away the property of their posterity? Surely
you ought not to condemn America.

On July 15, 1779, Benjamin and Charity bore their first
and only child, whom they named Clement Clarke Moore.
He was born at the Clarkes' Chelsea estate, although

Benjamin and Charity established their own home in Elmhurst, Queens. Benjamin continued his studies, and a decade after Clement was born received his doctorate from Columbia College.

King's College, 1770

By 1800, his predecessor at Trinity, Samuel Provost, resigned to become Bishop of New York, and Benjamin was made Rector of Trinity. A year later, he was named the ninth bishop in the Episcopal Church of the United States of America, and was consecrated in St. Michael's Church, Trenton, New Jersey. That same year, Benjamin was elected the third president of Columbia College. He was now among the most powerful men in New York City, and certainly one of its most prominent.

On July 11, 1804, Moore was summoned to the deathbed of Alexander Hamilton. Hamilton had been fatally shot in a duel with former friend and compatriot Aaron Burr. It was Hamilton's request to receive holy communion.

Moore objected for two reasons: first, Moore insisted it was a mortal sin to participate in a duel, and second, despite being a devout Christian in his later years, Hamilton was not an Episcopalian. Moore attempted to withdraw, but Hamilton's friends prevailed upon Moore to reconsider. Hamilton assured Moore that he was, in fact, repentant for taking part in the duel. Moore relented, and gave Hamilton communion.

In 1815, Bishop Provost died, and Moore was installed as the second bishop of New York. Moore's reign was short, however, for he died the following year in Greenwich Village, on February 27, 1816. He was buried in the Trinity Church cemetery, not too far from the grave of Alexander Hamilton. It was ironic, of course, that Trinity was also the final resting place of Walter Livingston, a close relative of Henry Livingston Jr.

To say that Clement Clarke Moore was born into a world of privilege is an understatement.

"Clement Clarke Moore was one of the most fortunate of men. He was born to culture and the means to sustain it. He would have been happy in the Renaissance and pleased to know Cosimo the Elder," wrote Moore's biographer Samuel W. Patterson. "Young Moore had no need to worry about employment for financial return. As an only child he enjoyed everything, especially those finer things of life, which a devoted family in a rural society willingly and generously provided."

"Clement Clarke Moore spent much of his boyhood and youth at his grandparents' estate in Elmhurst, then known as Newtown," wrote the New York journalist Judy Close. "The plot of land is now the site of the Moore Homestead Playground, near Broadway and 83rd Street, Elmhurst."

Moore homestead

It was a sturdy home, with large windows and straight lines, an ornate front door, and a front porch. From the front, the house issued two extensions, one more cottage-like and overgrown with ivy, the other jutting out with the final chimney of the four the house sported.

"Moore's earliest schooling was at home under his father's wise tutelage and even wiser guidance," according to Patterson. "The elder Moore was strict and thorough; Clement acquired a firm command of the tools of learning, which stood him in good stead to the end of his life." Later, "he might have prepared at the Columbia Grammar School where the standards were at least as high as at the older Boston Latin School."

Clement went on to attend Columbia College, which George II had established as King's College in 1754 through a royal charter. With the onset of the Revolution and the occupation of New York by the British, classes were suspended until the British vacated the city in 1783. The state reconstituted the school and insisted the name be changed to Columbia College. In 1787, John Jay and Alexander Hamilton, an alumnus, headed a committee to revise the school's charter. Emphasis was on the liberal arts through the mid-19th century. As Nathaniel Fish Moore, a professor and later president of the college, wrote to his cousin Clement, "The old paths are those in which she still ought to walk... for the duties of life, and for the attainment of a blessed and glorious existence hereafter."

Mathematics, natural philosophy, moral philosophy, rhetoric, belle-lettres, classics, chemistry, and languages (French, Hebrew, Latin) were the common core of the day. Though Clement dabbled in chemistry briefly, he was drawn to classics. He graduated in May 6, 1789, first in his class (as was his father a generation before). President George Washington and Vice President John Adams were both in attendance as Clement delivered his valedictory speech "Grati-tude." Moore then earned his master's degree in 1801 from the same institution.

Moore's earliest known written work was a pro-Feder-alist pamphlet that he published in 1804 as a rejoinder to Thomas Jefferson's famous *Notes on the State of Virginia*. In the book, Jefferson stated his thoughts on the separation of church and state, constitutional government, checks and balances, and individual liberty. Jefferson railed against slavery, discussing miscegenation and the differences in the great racial divide.

On the latter subjects, Jefferson wrote of racial politics, "It will probably be asked, Why not retain and incorporate the blacks into the state, and thus save the expense of sup-plying, by importation of white settlers, the vacancies they will leave? Deep rooted prejudices entertained by the whites; ten thousand recollections, by the blacks, of the injuries they have sustained; new provocations; the real distinctions which nature has made; and many other circumstances, will divide us into parties, and produce convulsions, which will probably never end but in the extermination of the one or the other race."

At the time of its publication, 1785, it was incendiary and provocative. It was also considered one of the best books written by an American before 1800. But in 1804, Jefferson was running for reelection as President of the United States, and Moore was appalled by Jefferson's liberal views.

Moore published his retort anonymously, titling it "Observations upon Certain Passages in Mr. Jefferson's Notes on Virginia: Which Appear to Have a Tendency to Subvert Religion, and Establish a False Philosophy." Moore called Jefferson's work an "instrument of infidelity."

"Moore was particularly anxious that Thomas Jefferson's views on the Bible might not prevail in America," according to Samuel Patterson.

Stephen Nissenbaum, a Fulbright visiting professor, a National Endowment for the Humanities fellow, and a scholar of early American history, defended Moore, writing, "Moore was socially and politically conservative, to be sure, but his conservatism was high Federalist, not low fundamentalist. He had the misfortune to come into adulthood at the turn of the nineteenth century, a time when old-style patricians were feeling profoundly out of place in Jeffersonian America. Moore's early prose publications are all attacks on the vulgarities of the new bourgeois culture that was taking control of the nation's political, economic, and social life, and which he (in tandem with others of his sort) liked to discredit with the term 'plebeian.'"

Still, when reading the young Moore's work, it comes across as a bit pious and lacking in humor. He could be haughty and judgmental, although he was never rude or mean because of his Christian faith and goodwill. No matter where he was, he was seen as kindly and quiet. He was always last to speak, if he spoke at all, and as he grew older, he grew to be a peacemaker, always eschewing confrontation, often seeking a gentler way to resolve conflict. He was always careful in his appearance and his manner, which some may have thought off-putting, comporting himself as a patrician of his class.

In his lifetime, Moore wrote other anonymous pamphlets, including an argument against the War of 1812 ("A Sketch of Our Political Condition. Addressed to the Citizens of the United States, Without Distinction of Party. By a Citizen of New-York") and a few years later an argument against the proposed urban planning of the city of New York ("A Plain Statement, Addressed to the Proprietors of Real Estate, in the City and County of New-York. By A Landholder"). The city planner had mapped out a north-south avenue that cut

Chelsea estate

through the Chelsea estate. Moore had to rip out groves of trees and tear down fences at his own expense. Later he received a tax bill from the city: his estate had been assessed within the city's limits. "Private convenience must give way to public good," he lamented. Neither pamphlet made much of a splash.

Moore's bigger accomplishment was his book, published in 1809, *A Compendius Lexicon of the Hebrew Language* in two volumes. Like his pamphlets, it did not set the world

Complete Treatise
on Merinos *title page*

ablaze, but it was a very respectable work as a vocabulary builder for beginners. Moore was an authority on language—Hebrew, Greek and Latin. He knew French and German as well, and had also studied Italian. In 1811, his name was affixed to a translation from the French of *A Complete Treatise on Merinos and Other Sheep*. This was not without its confusion. "It is a compilation by a French author, Alexandre Henri Tessier," advised Moore's biographer Patterson. "The work poses a problem and raises a question."

"About the turn of the nineteenth century, Major Henry's wealthy cousin Robert L. Livingston imported from Spain a flock of Merino sheep. In 1809 he published a book called 'An Essay on Sheep...An Account of the Merinos of

Spain,' wrote the literary detective Donald W. Foster. "Two years later, New York's Economical Office School published a book with a similar title..." Livingston had introduced the sheep at his estate Clermont, only a short way north from his cousin Henry's Locust Grove.

Moore later donated a volume of his *Merinos* to the New York Historical Society, writing in his name on the page indicating it was "translated from the French." Foster wrote, "The professor donated this trifle to the library of the Historical Society as a sample of his work in French-English translation — a text not previously recognized as his own production, but there it was. Before inscribing the volume, Professor Moore ought to have read the book cover to cover."

"The problem concerns the appendix where Francis Durand is named as 'Proprietor and Translator,'" wrote Patterson. The copyright notice stated that Durand had filed for copyright on November 30, 1811, and was listed as the "sole translator." Patterson added, "Did merino or any other kind of sheep ever nibble the grass of Chelsea? We do not know."

Foster thought not. "The professor kept remarkably thorough financial records, from which there is no indication that he kept any livestock except for carriage horses. I doubt that Professor Moore ever came closer to a Merino sheep than roast mutton or woolen underwear."

Foster was not alone in this kind of thinking. The Merino sheep book had caused consternation for some time. Even Moore's own hagiographic biographer Samuel W. Patterson was confused by Moore's apparent attribution, writing, "He may have felt that he so thoroughly revised Durand's work to make it his own," he tried to reason.

Had Moore attempted to take credit for someone else's work? Or was it merely a clerical error? Had a well-intentioned librarian misunderstood, and wrongly attributed it to Moore? No one knows, but for generations the Historical Society's library ascribed the translation to Moore.

Moore married Catharine Elizabeth Taylor, the daughter of William and Elizabeth Taylor of Middletown, New Jersey, on November 20, 1813. Catharine's mother was a direct descendant of the Dutch Van Cortlandt family, one of the same families directly related to the Livingstons.

Fifteen years younger than Clement, Catharine "had a God given sense of humor," wrote Patterson. Moore had been absolutely spellbound by the young woman. While he had spurned more adventuresome women in the past and had forgone balls and parties, being the bookish student he was, he wrote fanciful verse for Catharine. She was as taken with him as he was with her.

Her contemporaries could not understand her attraction to the pious, middle-aged bookworm, nor could her family. So Catharine wrote a poem titled "Clement C. Moore — My Reasons for Loving."

"Simple, adolescent charm is in every line; love and pride in her choice unaffectedly glow in word upon word," wrote Patterson.

The couple produced nine children: Margaret Elliott Moore (1815-1845), Charity Elizabeth Moore (1816-1830), Benjamin Moore (1818-1886), Mary Clarke Moore (1819-1893), Clement Moore (1821-1889), Emily Moore (1822-1828), William Taylor Moore (1823-1897), Katharine Van Cortlandt Moore (1826-1890), and Maria Theresa Moore (1826-1897).

During the raising of his family, Moore seemed to soften. The appearance of children filled him with sagacity. He grew to be a more understanding human being, publishing less vitriolic work, and even discovering a more playful side of himself. He was never the dashing, outgoing, bon vivant that Livingston was, but the experience of living with children seemed to relax the seemingly stodgy professor.

While Clement's father had always wanted him to become a priest like himself, Clement chose the academic life, albeit with a strong tie to religion. In 1821, Moore was made Professor of Biblical Learning and Interpretation of Scripture at the Diocesan Seminary of New York. After that school merged with another, in 1823 he joined the faculty of

Desmond Tutu Center at the
General Theological Seminary

the General Theological Seminary, where he was professor of Oriental and Greek literature until his retirement in 1850. From 1840 to 1850, Moore also served as a board member of the New York Institution for the Blind at 34th Street and Ninth Avenue. Moore was also a board member for the New York Institution of the Blind from 1840 to 1850, which used to be located on Ninth Avenue and 34th Street. Founded in 1831, the school is now known as The New York Institute for Special Education and is located on Pelham Parkway in the Bronx.

Throughout his life, Moore's faith grew stronger and stronger, his values more and more tied to the Anglican Church. He continued to involve himself with many church activities across the city. This eventually led him back to a stronger association with the religious life of his childhood.

The pious Moore nevertheless

Seminary Chapel

owned several slaves, as did many wealthy landowners of the day. After the Revolution, New York passed a law in 1799, gradually abolishing slavery in the state. According to the legislation, there were to be no slaves in the state after 1827. Being a pastor however, did not keep Moore from being a staunch anti-abolitionist well up to the time of the Civil War.

Clement was very active in the church life of the city. The first church he helped to establish was the Church of St. Luke in the Fields, which was an Episcopal church that can still be found at 487 Hudson Street in Greenwich Village. Moore helped organize the establishing of this church through Trinity Church. It marked a pivotal moment in his life. The completed church and grounds for the new church proved to set the standard for urban churches for some time to come.

Built in 1821–22 by contractors John Heath and James N. Wells, the Federalist-styled red brick build-

Church of St. Luke in the Fields

ing with its large square tower resembled an English village church. Moore himself laid out the complex of the church and its surrounding area, and then accepted the role of being the church's first pastor.

"In the 1820's Clement Clarke Moore took up full-time residence in his old summer house near 23d Street and Ninth Avenue, then at the center of his family's large estate. It was there that in 1822, as development was beginning to move up from Greenwich Village," wrote Christopher Gray in *The New York Times*, "Wells began to advise Moore on the development of what is now known as Chelsea."

This was a very busy time for Moore, with his many responsibilities and a growing family. It was during these many years of the development of Chelsea that his wife Catharine Elizabeth Taylor Moore died on April 4, 1830. "He was the widowed father of a large and growing family bereft of a mother who had taken much of the care and discipline of the household from his shoulders. His children, three of them boys, claimed a good deal of his time and attention," wrote Patterson. But the planning of the new Manhattan neighborhood took up more and more of Clement's time.

"Wells became Moore's property manager and developed the rather sophisticated restrictions that Moore imposed on his lots when private house construction began in earnest in the mid-1830's. These covenants not only included prohibitions against stables and rear buildings, but also required tree planting. Clearly Moore and Wells were taking pains to create a first-class residential district," continued

Gray. Severe restrictions included what could or could not be built on the land as well as specific architectural details of the buildings, which Moore himself dictated.

Wells' buildings remain even today.

It was ironic that Moore insisted that the new neighborhood he was laying out with Wells, selling off one small parcel of land after another and pocketing the immense revenues, be lined with expensive brick buildings of the highest quality. Despite his protestations of a decade earlier, Moore now envisioned an expensive, well-heeled neighborhood and a prodigious bank account for himself and his family. Meanwhile, Wells built

444 West 22nd St., 1919

three or four little wooden structures on what today is Ninth Avenue and 21st Street that consisted of storefronts with rental units above. Those little wooden buildings still stand today! They are as unique and stand out as awkwardly today as much as they did back then. At the time, many builders and new owner-residents considered them an eyesore.

"On March 31, 1845, other Chelsea developers who were building on lots subject to Moore's restrictions complained to him about the frame buildings that Wells was building on 'that beautiful block of ground,' Ninth Avenue between 21st and 22nd Streets, calling them 'a climax of injustice' and demanding relief," Gray wrote. "Nineteenth-century developers often viewed such property restrictions as many current developers

444 West 22nd St., today

do the Landmarks Preservation Commission's rules, grateful for the overall control of their neighborhood but restive when their own freedom of action is restricted."

In the early 1820s, the General Theological Society was reestablished in New York City, with its mission to reflect the moderate-to-liberal consensus on moral and theological issues. The three men responsible for its return were John Pintard of the New-York Historical Society, Bishop Hobart, and Clement Moore. Moore began teaching at the school and also donated 66 tracts of land, his former apple orchard at Chelsea, for the organization's new home. Currently located on Ninth Avenue at the west end of 21st and 22nd streets, it remains the oldest seminary of the Episcopal Church and is a leading center of theological education.

According to Niels Henry Sonne, a noted librarian, rare-book curator, and expert on the Gutenberg Bible, "The Library of The General Theological Seminary is a magnificent treasury of books, manuscripts, records and source materials for the study of the life and thought of Christianity." John Pintard made the first donation, one of 2,500 volumes the library would acquire in the first year alone. J. H. Feltus was the first librarian. The Friends of the Library was established in 1834, and the endowment they created is still active and productive today. It was here that Moore remained a professor until 1850.

In the 1850s, Moore bought a summer place in the swanky summer seaside resort of Newport, Rhode Island. His home, located at the southwest corner of Catherine Street and Greenough Place, still stands and is today a small apartment building. The house is a popular tourist attraction, called by various names—Cedars, Clement C. Moore House, and The Night Before Christmas House. It is often incorrectly claimed as site of the composition of Moore's famous poem—that being, of course, 'Twas the Night Before Christmas.

Moore is most frequently the author to whom the poem

is ascribed. If so, it's unlikely that Newport provided the inspiration for the poem's setting. "Some historians believe his ca. 1661 ancestral Queens farmhouse and surrounding acreage was the setting Moore chose for his poem, inspired by his memory of childhood Christmases spent at his grandparents' Newtown home," wrote the journalist Judy Close.

Moore summered in Newport until his death on July 10, 1863. His funeral was held in Trinity Church, Newport, where he had purchased a pew. His body was returned to New York for burial in the cemetery at St. Luke in the Fields. On November 29, 1899, his body was reinterred in Trinity Church Cemetery and Mausoleum in New York at 155th Street and Riverside.

Moore published poetry throughout his career. He was quoted of writing poetry, "No production which assumes the guise of poetry ought to be tolerated, if it possesses no other recommendation than the glow of its expressions and

Clement C. Moore grave

the tinkling of its syllables...." In 1844, Bartlett & Wellford published his book *Poems*. In the preface, Moore wrote, "In compliance with your wishes, I here present you with a volume of verses, written by me, at different periods of my life." During his life he'd published in *The Evening Post*, *New-York Magazine*, *Literary Repository*, and others.

Of the poems in the collection, a portion are either translations or poems by his deceased wife. And many are traditional pieces written to other poets or authors such as Robert Southey and Robert Cowper.

"Dr. Moore's poetical talents incline him to domestic themes and incidents and characters; he is a disciple of Cowper and Goldsmith; yet by no means an imitator of either. His vein is original: his manner is his own—still, his admiration for classic models may guide his taste and control his pen," wrote William Alfred Jones in the *Literary World*, July 17, 1847.

Here are a few samples:

Lines

This name here drawn by Flora's hand
Portay's, alas! Her mind:
The beating surf and yielding sand
Soon leave no trace behind.

But Flora's name shall still abide
In many a bosom trac'd,
Not e'en by time's destroying tide
Nor fortune's storms effac'd.

Another was written in 1846:

To a very young lady who sent me a kiss.

Thousand thanks, my sweet girl, for the kiss that you sent!
And ten thousand times more for your heart's kind intent!
But, ah me! like a blossom too tender to last,
Ere it reach'd me, the freshness and fragrance were past.
There are kisses, 'tis true, may be sent where you choose;
But 'tis only because they've no sweetness to lose.
There are fruits which endure the approach of decay;
But the true zest of nature breathes fresh from the spray.
There are flowers, deep-tinted and rich of perfume,
That, when gather'd, awhile may continue to bloom;
But the flowrets of morn, breathing soft thro' the dew,
Lose their charms soon as pluck'd from the stem where
they grew.
There are wines of a spirit so rich and so sound,
They improve to the taste as they go the world round;
While the exquisite flavor of some is so faint

That the vessel containing them oft gives a taint.
Then, believe me, whenever your gifts you would send,
Never trust them in charge of the faithfulest friend;
For their worth can be told and their sweetness made
known
By no substitute's [h]and, by no lips but your own.

Of all the poems, only a few poems were written in the anapestic style—the same, sing-songy style as *'Twas the Night Before Christmas*. The most notable and enjoyable was *The Pig and the Rooster*, which Moore explained "was occasioned by a subject for composition given to the boys of a grammar school attended by one of my sons—viz: 'Which are to be preferred, the pleasures of a pig or a chicken?'"

The Pig and The Rooster

On a warm sunny day, in the midst of July,
A lazy young pig lay stretched out in his sty,
Like some of his betters, most solemnly thinking
That the best things on earth are good eating and drinking.
At length, to get rid of the gnats and the flies,
He resolv'd, from his sweet meditations to rise;
And, to keep his skin pleasant, and pliant, and cool,
He plung'd him, forthwith, in the next muddy pool.

When, at last, he thought fit to arouse from his bath,
A conceited young rooster came just in his path:
A precious smart prig, full of vanity drest,
Who thought, of all creatures, himself far the best.
"Hey day! little grunter, why where in the world
Are you going so perfum'd, pomatum'd and curl'd?
Such delicate odors my senses assail,
And I see such a sly looking twist to your tail,
That you, sure, are intent on some elegant sporting;
Hurra! I believe, on my life, you are courting;
And that figure which moves with such exquisite grace,
Combin'd with the charms of that soft-smiling face,
In one who's so neat and adorn'd with such art,
Cannot fail to secure the most obdurate heart.
And much joy do I wish you, both you and your wife,
For the prospect you have of a nice pleasant life."

"Well, said, Master Dunghill," cried Pig in a rage,
"You're, doubtless, the prettiest beau of the age,
With those sweet modest eyes staring out of your head,
And those lumps of raw flesh, all so bloody and red.
Mighty graceful you look with those beautiful legs,
Like a squash or a pumpkin on two wooden pegs.
And you've special good reason your own life to vaunt,
And the pleasures of others with insult to taunt;

Among cackling fools, always clucking or crowing,
And looking up this way and that way, so knowing,
And strutting and swelling, or stretching a wing,
To make you admired by each silly thing;
And so full of your own precious self, all the time,
That you think common courtesy almost a crime;
As if all the world was on the look out
To see a young rooster go scratching about."

Hereupon, a debate, like a whirlwind, arose,
Which seem'd fast approaching to bitings and blows;
'Mid squeaking and grunting, Pig's arguments flowing;
And Chick venting fury 'twixt screaming and crowing.
At length to decide the affair, 'twas agreed
That to counsellor Owl they should straightway proceed;
While each, in his conscience, no motive could show,
But the laudable wish to exult o'er his foe.
Other birds, of all feather, their vigils were keeping,
While Owl, in his nook, was most learnedly sleeping:
For, like a true sage, he preferred the dark night,
When engaged in his work, to the sun's blessed light.
Each stated his plea, and the owl was required
To say whose condition should most be desired.
It seemed to the judge a strange cause to be put on,
To tell which was better, a fop or a glutton;

Yet, like a good lawyer, he kept a calm face,
And proceeded, by rule, to examine the case;
With both his round eyes gave a deep-meaning wink,
And, extending one talon, he set him to think.
In fine, with a face much inclin'd for a joke,
And a mock solemn accent, the counsellor spoke –
"'Twixt Rooster and Roaster, this cause to decide,
Would afford me, my friends, much professional pride.
Were each on the table serv'd up, and well dress'd,
I could easily tell which I fancied the best;
But while both here before me, so lively I see,
This cause is, in truth, too important for me;
Without trouble, however, among human kind,
Many dealers in questions like this you may find,
Yet, one sober truth, ere we part, I would teach –
That the life you each lead is best fitted for each.
'Tis the joy of a cockerel to strut and look big,
And to wallow in mire, is the bliss of a pig.
But, whose life is more pleasant, when viewed in itself,
Is a question had better be laid on the shelf,
Like many which puzzle deep reasoners' brains,
And reward them with nothing but words for their pains.
So now, my good clients, I have been long awake,
And I pray you, in peace, your departure to take.
Let each one enjoy, with content, his own pleasure,

> *Nor attempt, by himself, other people to measure."*
> *Thus ended the strife, as does many a fight;*
> *Each thought his foe wrong, and his own notions right.*
> *Pig turn'd, with a grunt, to his mire anew,*
> *And He-biddy, laughing, cried — Cock-a-doodle-doo.*

"There runs through all Professor Moore's verse a kind of frustration," Vassar president Henry Noble MacCracken wrote in 1958. "He feels he should be a greater man than he is, a greater poet. The public did not agree with him, even about his poetry. His friends tried to get him to relax, but he never let down his moral guard. Dr. Willy Bard tried to get him to come to a dance, but Moore answered the famous physician in a surly poem. He was a self-torturing Midas; all around him was a rich harvest of poetry, which he turned to lead."

Even James Thurber of *The New Yorker* fame wrote about Moore's poems, opining, "Dr. Moore loved to write. His chief literary work is a ponderous book entitled 'A Compendious Lexicon of the Hebrew Language.' He also liked to turn out pieces such as one called 'Observations upon Certain Passages in Mr. Jefferson's Note on the State of Virginia which Appear to have a Tendency to Subvert Religion and Establish a False Philosophy.' In 1836 he published a volume of verses. The best of the lot was "Twas the Night

Before Christmas.' There was only one other in the same metre (anapaestic) and it was not so good."

But nowhere in his papers was the original *Night Before Christmas* poem ever produced. In fact, no copies of it exist in his hand even prior to its being ascribed to him in 1837 by the literary aggregator and editor Charles Fenno Hoffmann. Nothing. It wasn't until 1844, after he had already claimed it, that he volunteered that he had supplied it to Hoffman. But there remains no correspondence between the two to prove it.

The earliest handwritten version of the poem exists in the New Brunswick Museum, in Canada. In the museum's archives exists the correspondence and papers of the Odell family. The museum's website reads, "There is a handwritten version of 'A visit from St. Nicholas.' It was written in 1825, and very likely the handwriting is that of Jonathan Odell's daughter Maryl. The Odell family were Loyalists who came to New Brunswick from New York in 1784 and the Moore and Odell families were friends in pre-revolutionary times. Jonathan Odell was the first Provincial Secretary of New Brunswick and was Clement Moore's godfather. The families continued to correspond in the decades after the Odells left New York."

The poem had been an instant success, and was reprinted many times far and wide by 1825. There was no evidence the poem had been sent by any member of the Moore family. And it had been copied after the poem's publication. Had Maryl copied the poem after seeing it in a local or regional paper? No one knows.

And the story gets murkier from there.

CHAPTER 5

Attribution to Moore

The note that accompanied the poem in the *Troy Sentinel* on December 23, 1823 was written by the newspaper's editor, Orville L. Holley. We saw a portion of this note in the first chapter of this book. Here is how the complete note read:

> *We know not to whom we are indebted for the following description of that unwearied patron of children — that homely, but delightful personification of parental kindness — SANTE CLAUS, his costume and his equipage, as he goes about vis-*

iting the fire-sides of this happy land, laden with Christmas bounties; but, from whomsoever it may have come, we give thanks for it. There is, to our apprehension, a spirit of cordial goodness in it, a playfulness of fancy, and a benevolent alacrity to enter into the feelings and promote the simple pleasures of children, which are altogether charming. We hope our little patrons, both lads and lasses, will accept it as proof of our un-feigned good will toward them – as a token of our warmest wish that they may have many a merry Christmas; that they may long retain their beautiful relish for those unbought, homebred joys, which derive their flavor from filial piety and fraternal love, and which they may be assured are the least-alloyed that time can furnish them; and that they may never part with that simplicity of character, which is their own fairest ornament, and for the sake of which they have been pronounced, by au-thority which one can gainsay, the types of such as shall inherit the kingdom of heaven.

"The fifty-six line poem was such an instant success with readers that for several years the Sentinel reprinted it each Christmas and about 1830 began issuing it as a broadside, with a woodcut by Myron King showing Santa sailing over rooftops in this sleigh. The sheet was handed out by carriers when they delivered the paper's Christmas edition," wrote Martin Gardiner, the author of *The Annotated Night Before*

Myron King woodcut, 1830

Christmas. Indeed, the poem had found fame all by itself, and began reprinting elsewhere, including the *New Brunswick* (New Jersey) *Almanac, for the Year of Our Lord 1825.* "Not until seven years later was the question raised about the poem's origin," continued Gardiner. "Who was the author, the New York Courier wanted to know, when it printed the ballad on January 1, 1829. On January 20, Holley answered the question:

'*A few days since the editors of the New York Courier, at the request of a lady, inserted some lines descriptive of one of the Christmas visits of that good old Dutch saint, St. Nicholas, and at the same time applied to our Albany neighbors for information as to the author. That information, we apprehend, the Albany editors cannot give. The lines were first published in this paper. They came to us from a manuscript in possession of a lady in this city. We have been given to understand that the author of them belongs by birth and residence to the city of New York, and that he is a gentleman of more merit as a scholar and a writer than many of more noisy pretensions. We republish the lines in a preceding column just as they originally*

appeared, because we still think of them as at first, and for the
satisfaction of our brethren of the Courier, one of whom, at
least, is an Arcadian.'"

It was intimated at this point that the poem was the
work of Moore. "Holley's italicizing of more in his last sen-
tence, and his use of more two more times, suggests that he
knew who the author was, but respected Moore's desire not
to have his name associated with what he considered insig-
nificant doggerel," wrote Gardiner.

Holley never disclosed the poet's actual name and Moore
never attached his to it. The popularity and reputation of
the poem itself continued to grow. In the same year as the
Sentinel's holiday broadside, the first abridgment appeared
in John F. Watson's *Annals of Philadelphia*. Two years after
that, in 1832, among the many reprintings of the poem
during the holiday season, the Schenectady Whig replaced
the poem's original "Happy Christmas..." with the ever more
popular "Merry Christmas."

"In the 1836 item below, transcribed from the Ontar-
io Repository and Freeman (Canandaigua, New York), the
same editor Orville L. Holley states that he learned of the
author's true identity only months, not years, after printing
the poem in the Troy Sentinel," wrote Scott Norsworthy in
the blog "Melvilliana."

'SANTA CLAUS, WITH HIS CHRISTMAS GIFTS.

The following lines appeared in print for the first time – though very often copied since – in the Troy Sentinel of December 23, 1823, which paper we then conducted. They were introduced, on that occasion, with the following remarks; which, as they continue to be a true expression of our opinion of the charming simplicity and cordiality of the lines, as well as of our unchanged feelings toward the little people to whom they are addressed, we repeat them, only observing that although when we first published them, we did not know who wrote them, yet, not many months afterwards we learnt that they came from the pen of a most accomplished scholar and an estimable man, a professor in one of our colleges....'

– found at NYS Historic Newspapers. This item was reprinted the following week in the Auburn Journal and Advertiser on Wednesday, January 4, 1837."

Still, however, Moore did not claim the poem. At all. And there are no extent notes, nor letters, nor diaries from the period that connect Moore to the poem at all. Not even privately that we know of. According to the auction house Sotheby's, "Moore, who perhaps believed the light tone of the poem to be at odds with his professional standing, did not acknowledge authorship of the poem...."

By now, *A Visit from St. Nicholas* was among one of the

most revered poems in America. It was reprinted faithfully in dozens of newspapers in the Hudson Valley and as far west as Ohio and Missouri.

"The Visit from St. Nicholas is a little masterpiece of juvenile poetry. It is one of the best poems for children ever written. It begins and ends with children. Everything is designed in miniature. Mamma and papa are mere spectators. Mamma even disappears altogether after the first mention. But who cares? Papa is only a reporter of the sight, not a sharer," wrote Vassar president Henry Noble MacCracken in 1958 in his book *Blithe Dutchess: The Flowering of an American County from 1812.* "Children love motion, and the Visit is all motion. Papa flies to the window. The reindeer fly, too. So do the dry leaves. Santa Claus is all action, though no words. The adjectives all suggest childhood. Snug, rosy, jolly, happy, quick, are all in the child's world. So is the up and down, the on and away, of the reindeer. The tempo is that of the happy child, who must run to express his excitement. It is this breathless quality that gives speed to the rhythm of the anapaestic gallop. Only two images give even a hint of the adult point of view; the dry leaves blown aloft by the wild hurricane; and the midday lustre of a clear moonlight in snow. Both are novel and new, but not beyond a child's observation."

The poem continued to gather popular attention.

Charles Fenno Hoffman

Enter, then, one Charles Fenno Hoffman, a friend of Moore's and the son of New York Attorney General Josiah Ogden Hoffman. Like Moore, he attended Columbia College and also studied law, later being admitted to the New York bar in 1827, at the age of nineteen. But the law was not to be his life's profession. He was of a literary bent, and in 1833 he helped to establish *The Knickerbocker* magazine, which he edited. In 1836, he accepted the position of editor of the *New York Mirror* newspaper.

Hoffman published his first book in 1835, *A Winter in the Far West*, about his adventures in the Missouri Territory. He also published an adventure novel that same year, as well as *The New-York Book of Poetry*, which he edited.

It was Charles Fenno Hoffman who first included the poem in his collection. *A Visit from St. Nicholas* was at that time easily one of the most well-known of published American verses. Hoffman could scarcely publish his major anthology without its inclusion. It was Hoffman who first attributed it in print to his friend Moore. It was lumped in with other poems by Moore, including "To A Lady," "From a Father to His Children," and "From a Husband to His Wife."

No correspondence of any kind has been found in accordance with its inclusion. And Moore still did little to encourage the belief that he had written the lines. But nor is there any evidence that he attempted to disown it.

Several years later, the poem was attributed to the deceased Washington, D.C., artist Joseph Wood.

Daily National Intelligencer *masthead*

"It started with a mistaken attribution in the Washington [D. C.] Daily National Intelligencer, which prompted the New York American eventually to ask for a published correction," according to Norsworthy. "On December 25, 1843 the National Intelligencer published 'A Visit from St. Nicholas' with the following letter, dated December 22, 1843:

'GENTLEMEN: *The enclosed lines were written by JO-SEPH WOOD, artist, for the National Intelligencer, and published in that paper in 1827 or 1828, as you may perceive from your files. By republishing them as the composition of Mr. WOOD you will gratify one who now has few sources of pleasure left. Perhaps you may comply with this request, if it be only for "auld lange syne."'"*

According to Norsworthy, three days later the *Daily National Intelligencer* published this correction:

> *National Intelligencer — December 28, 1843*
>
> *Messrs. EDITORS: I perceive in your paper of the 25th instant that an extract from the beautiful little poem entitled "A Visit from St. Nicholas" is given to the pen of Jos. Wood. This is a mistake. It is well known to be the production of CLEMENT C. MOORE, of the city of New York, and is published as his in the volume of American Poems edited by John Keese. Very respectfully, &c.*
>
> *C.*

According to Norsworthy, "Subsequently the editor of the New York American must have urged the National Intelligencer editor to reprint 'a note of Mr. CLEMENT C. MOORE concerning the authorship of the admired lines of his.' The Washington, D.C. editor replied in essence that his paper had already made the desired correction, alluding to the letter from 'C.' that had appeared in the National Intelligencer on December 28, 1843."

Moore claimed not to know how the poem had made its way to the *Troy Sentinel*.

It was not until many years later, in 1871, that it was discovered, or disclosed, how *A Visit from St. Nicholas* arrived on Holley's desk. On December 23, 1871, one John T. Parker, a local citizen of Troy whose extensive family dated back to pre-Revolutionary times, attempted to set the record straight. Owing to the sketchiness of some of the details, he may have heard the story secondhand. Parker wrote to the *Troy Daily Times*:

> *Presuming you will publish, as usual, the "Visit of St. Nicholas," quoted above, I send you the enclosed history of it for the benefit of the young Trojans who sleep with one eye open on the night before Christmas. As it has a Trojan birth, it may interest even the editor to hear its narrative as related by me. In the year 1825, I think, the eldest daughter of Rev. David Butler, first rector of St. Paul's church, Miss Harriet Butler, on a visit to Prof. Clement C. Moore of Columbia College, New York, found on the centre table this "Visit of St. Nicholas," composed by the Professor for his children. Miss B. brought it to Troy with her, and gave a copy of it to O. I. Holley, the editor of the Troy Sentinel, published by Norman Tuttle. It took like wildfire, and was copied through the state. The Troy Sentinel printed it for the news boys for several years on Christmas day. Myron King executed a beautiful wood cut, representing St. Nicholas on his sleigh, drawn by six reindeer prancing up a steep house-top, and entering the chimney with his presents. In proof of its popular character, I have before*

me a beautiful copy of "American Poets," printed in London,
and the first poem is the "Visit of St. Nicholas" — a deserved
compliment to the country and author. Wishing you and yours
a right merry Christmas, Mr. Editor, I remain yours,
  John T. Parker

This was probably an apocryphal story, considering it had been almost fifty years after the fact.

Several literary historians have taken a crack at deciphering the real story. The first marker is a response from the original publisher of the *Troy Sentinel*, Norman Tuttle, whose letter was found among the Moore papers in the Museum of the City of New York. Note that Tuttle is responding to a letter he received from Moore a few days earlier. In his letter, Moore asked about the changing of the words Donder and Blixem (Dutch words for thunder and lightning) to Donner and Blitzen.

Troy. Feb 26. 1844.
Prof C C Moore,

Sir — Yours of 23d inst. making inquiry concerning the pub-
lication of "A Visit from St. Nicholas," is just received. The
piece was first published in the Troy Sentinel December 23,
1823, with an introductory notice by the Editor, Orville L.

Holley, Esq., and again two or three years after that. At the time of its first publication I did not know who the Author was — but have since been informed that you were the Author. I understand from Mr. Holley that he received it from Mrs. Sackett, the wife of Mr. Daniel Sackett who was then a merchant in this city. It was twice published in the Troy Sentinel; and being much admired and sought after by the younger class, I procured the Engraving which you will find on the other side of this sheet, and have published several editions of it. The Sentinel has for several years been numbered with the things that were — and Mr. Holley, I understand, is now in Albany, editing the Albany Daily Advertiser. I was myself the proprietor of the Sentinel.

Very Respectfully
Yours, &c
N Tuttle

According to Norsworthy, "Any sequence of transmission involving the Butlers, Sacketts, and Holley seems plausible. The families of Clement C. Moore and the Rev. David Butler were connected through longstanding ties of friendship and religion. Rev. Butler was then rector of St. Paul's Episcopal Church in Troy (consecrated in 1806 by Moore's father, the Bishop). Butler in turn was socially and political-

Tuttle to Moore letter

ly connected with Daniel Sackett and Orville Holley as leading citizens of Troy, and prominent Whigs. All three were founding members of the Troy Colonization Society."

But Norsworthy felt that Moore's February 23 letter to Tuttle "gave the lie to the Butler story. Before publishing the poem as his own, Clement Moore apparently had made sure that his claim to the poem as his own would not be challenged."

Norsworthy also found a published letter from Moore to Charles King, the editor of the *Washington National Intelligencer*, "in which Moore corrects a mistaken attribution of his poem 'A Visit from St. Nicholas.' Writing from New York on February 27, 1844, Moore responds to a December 22, 1843 item in the Washington National Intelligencer that falsely attributed the already well-known Christmas poem to the deceased artist Joseph Wood. Moore's chagrined friend Charles King published the letter on March 1, 1844 and requested the *National Intelligencer* to remedy the 'plagiarism' by reprinting 'Mr. Moore's note' of correction. The *National Intelligencer* reply on March 6, 1844 is what led me to

look for Moore's published claim of authorship. In answer
to Charles King's complaint, the editor of the Intelligencer
pointed out that his newspaper had promptly published a
correction, so there was no need to reprint Moore's letter."

From the *New York American*, March 1, 1844:

*LINES TO ST. NICHOLAS. — The following note from
our friend C. C. Moore, the author of those lines which every
child among us delights to hear, about Christmas, and which
parents with not less delight recite, brings to our notice, one of
the boldest acts of plagiarism of which we have any recollec-
tion. We ask the National Intelligencer to have the goodness
to insert Mr. Moore's note—and if possible to elucidate the
mistake, if such it be, or fraud attempted in respect of such
well known lines.*

New York, Feb. 27, 1844

*Dear Sir—My attention was, a few days ago, directed
to the following communication, which appears in the
National Intelligencer of the 25th of December last.
"Washington, Dec. 22d, 1843.*

Gentlemen—

*The enclosed lines were written by Joseph Wood,
artist, for the National Intelligencer, and published in
that paper in 1827 or 1828, as you may perceive from
your files. By republishing them, as the composition of*

Mr. Wood you will gratify one who has now few sources of pleasure left. Perhaps you may comply with this request, if it be only for 'auld lang syne.'"

The above is printed immediately over some lines, describing a visit from St. Nicholas, which I wrote many years ago, I think somewhere between 1823 and 1824, not for publication, but to amuse my children. They, however, found their way, to my great surprise, in the Troy Sentinel: nor did I know, until lately, how they got there. When "The New York Book" was about to be published, I was applied to for some contribution to the work. Accordingly, I gave the publisher several pieces, among which was the "Visit from St. Nicholas." It was printed under my name, and has frequently since been republished, in your paper among others, with my name attached to it.

Under these circumstances, I feel it incumbent on me not to remain silent, while so bold a claim, as the above quoted, is laid to my literary property, however small the intrinisic [sic] value of that property may be. The New York Book was published in 1827 [1837].

Yours, truly and respectfully,

CLEMENT C. MOORE

Chas. King, Esq.

Norsworthy wrote, "The 'New York Book' to which Moore refers is of course the 1837 *New-York Book of Poetry*, edited by Moore's friend (and some years later, Herman Melville's friend) Charles Fenno Hoffman."

It was clear that Moore was scrupulously following up the trail of publication before enforcing his own claim to the poem. A claim he would stake emphatically when he published his own book of poetry in 1844, including in it "A Visit from St. Nicholas."

According to Winthrop P. Tryon, writing in *The Christian Science Monitor*, "A name for the first time was definitely fixed to it in the public prints late in 1838, when the Troy [New York] Budget, in the course of editorial comment, referred to Clement C. Moore, the Hebrew scholar, of New York, as the person who had written it." Thus the ball began to roll in favor of Moore as being the

Poems *title page*

acknowledged author of the poem. Momentum from this point continued to gather.

Much, much later in life, Moore told of the writing of the poem, explaining that on a snowy Christmas Eve, in 1822, his young wife "Catharine sent her husband out into the elements to get one more turkey, which she and the children were preparing as a donation to the poor. Their home, with six children at the time, was one filled with love and warmth and tradition," according to Jeff Westover, who writes frequently on aspects of Christmas. "Clement ventured into town, his coachman being a jolly, round fellow with a long white beard and a most cheerful disposition. After he purchased the needed turkey from Jefferson's Market, with sleigh bells merrily ringing in his ears as the snow fell that Christmas Eve day, he composed a short poem. Moore returned home with the turkey and the family traditions of Christmas took hold. He added to them by delighting his young children that night by the fire with the first reading of 'The Night Before Christmas,' the poem he had composed that very afternoon. Then, he tucked his handwritten copy of his creation away and gave it no further thought."

On December 20, 1920, in New York City, Maria Jephson O'Conor (née Post), said, "My grandfather, Elliot Taylor was a brother-in-law of Clement C. Moore; his daughter Maria Farquahar Taylor married my late father Colonel Henry C. Post. Under these circumstances my father became well acquainted with the above Clement C. Moore. He related to me the manner in which Dr Moore told him the little poem entitled 'A visit from St Nicholas' came to be written....On his return with the turkey he was struck with the beauty of the moonlight on the snow and the brightness of the starlit sky. This, with the holiday season, suggested to him the idea of writing a few lines appropriate to St. Nicholas. He also told my father when the same was published, without his knowledge, that there were only two errors in the printed copy."

That was the story of the writing of the poem. And it would stick for many years. Moore had cemented the ownership of the poem for the rest of his life, and for perhaps, all time. But even in his lifetime, more than a few people were considered likely candidates to have written the verses as well.

CHAPTER 6

The Objections of Henry Livingston Jr.'s Family

As late as 1860, *A Visit from St. Nicholas* was still being published in newspapers, literary magazines, and journals all over the country. An excellent example was the *Art Journal*, a literary magazine of note. *A Visit* was already one of America's favorite poems. But few knew, or cared, who wrote it. But there were a few....

While Moore had claimed the poem and had only as recently as 1844 started remedying his absenteeism over the poem, he was of such minor importance as a poet in the literary world that his book *Poems*, where he had included it, was unfindable. Only a chosen few within his rarified scholarly and literary New York City circle were familiar with it.

It was in 1860 when the Livingstons first heard of the Clement C. Moore claim from a relative, Eliza Clement Brewer Livingston. Jeanne Hubbard Denig, another Livingston relative, related the story: "Grandmother was greatly exercised [sic] when the first printed Xmas copy appeared (I have it.) and said there was a mistake that should be rectified. That Henry Livingston wrote the verses," wrote Denig many years later of the incident, in 1917. "This is my only proof. The word of my stately, truthful, dependable grandmother, Eliza Clement Brewer Livingston. I could go on — but enough — "

Still, the Livingston clan persisted. On January 3, 1900, Cornelia Griswold Goodrich wrote to Henry Livingston of Babylon, Long Island.

Mr. Henry Livingston,
Dear Sir,

In the "Sun" of December 29th 1899 Mr. S.W. Cooper asks for a solution of the claim of Clement C. Moore to the authorship of "The Night before Xmas" and cites you as contesting the point.

I am a great-great-granddaughter of Major Henry Livingston of Po'keepsie, N.Y. and it is a long established belief in
our family that our great g. grandfather was the author. We
have many similar poems of his written in that vein, or rather
my cousin, Miss Gertrude Thomas has, whose Mother was a
daughter by the second wife of the said Henry Livingston. His
son Edwin Livingston had the original poem in manuscript
and prized it very highly but it was destroyed in a fire when out
West with all his household articles. He and all his brothers
and sisters remember distinctly their father coming from out his
"den" as he called his study in the old Manor House at Locust
Grove on the South Road two miles out of Po'keepsie and long
since the property of my Uncle, Prof. S.F.B. Morse, and reading
this poem to his children just before Xmas. I have letters in
my possession testifying to this, at the time the question was
asked in the daily papers about 25 years ago as to who was the
author of Mother Goose's Nursery Rhymes, and who the author of 'Twas the Night Before Xmas'. We could find no paper
in which it was published altho all his children remember its
having been published in a Po'keepsie paper at that time, between 1780 and 1800. They think the paper was called "The
Po'keepsie Gazette" tho it may have been the Knickerbocker
Mag; –

His children declare that the Moore's must have been possessed of the poem in the following manner; a young governess

was visiting in my g-g-grandfather's family at Locust Grove who was employed in the Moore family somewhere down South. She was a mutual friend of both families – At the time of her visit this poem had just been written and was read to her, she was much struck by it and asked for a copy and taking it down South after returning to the Moore family, no doubt it lay there for years without a claimant and no doubt minus a name, for in those days authors were more modest than they are now-a-days and names were not given the publicity they are at present. Clement C. Moore I think was dead when his children or g. children laid claim to this poem, and I don't think either C.C. Moore himself or any of his family would knowingly lay claim to anything that was not their own, did they think it belonged to another, but in the lapse of years, a poem lying about without a name, you can easily conceive how easily it could be transferred. We have as you see, no actual proof, no mss, only the actual eye-witnesses of the birth of this charming poem on the spot and at the time I indicate, and I am sure 5 people out of a family could not have been so positive were there not truth in the assertion.

Office of "The Signal,"
A Local Paper for Live People Independent in Politics
Impartial in Religion "Square" in Business
HENRY LIVINGSTON, SON & CO.
Proprietors and Editors.
Babylon, N.Y., Jan. 10, 1900
Cornelia G. Goodrich

Dear Friend:

I was surprised and pleased to receive your letter, written (or at least postmarked) Jan 3, 1900.

The question of the authorship of the poem "The Night Before Christmas" was never brought up, to my knowledge, until after 1862, when it was published and credited to Clement C. Moore. Moore was then a very old man, and died the same year. It does not appear, however, that he ever laid claim to the authorship, and it is said he was displeased at first when it was attributed to him!

My father, (Sidney Montgomery) as long ago as I can remember, claimed that his father (Henry, Jr.) was the author: that it was first read to the children at the old homestead below Poughkeepsie, when he was about eight years old, which would be about 1804, or 1805. He had the original manuscript, with many corrections in his possession, for a long time, and by him was given to his brother Edwin. Edwin's personal effects were destroyed when his sister Susan's home was burned at Kaskaskia, Wis., about 1847 or 8.

I think the poem was first published in the Knickerbocker Magazine early in this century, but whether the author's name was attached or not I do not know. The Magazine is on file in the Astor Library, & some time I mean to hunt it up— If I find it as I expect I will certainly inform you. I thank you most heartily for your kindly letter. Wish you every happiness, I am truly yours,

Henry Livingston

Indeed, the Livingstons were energized by the realization that the poem they thought belonged to their family had been claimed by Moore. Searches through the old Major's papers and works began in earnest. Letters and reminiscences flew back and forth among the family and spilled into print. The earliest memories placed the poem as far back as 1804, based on family hearsay. It would seem unlikely, however, that Livingston would have written the poem that early. The myths that the poem were founded on had not yet been invented or evolved. And as with all things where time intervenes, memories get cloudy on both sides.

Dear Annie

Your letter has just reached me, and I hasten to tell you all I know about the poem 'Night Before Christmas.' It was approved and believed in our family to be Father's, and I well remember our astonishment when we saw it claimed as Clement C. Moore's.

Many years after my father's decease, which took place more than fifty years ago [1828]; at that time my brothers in looking over his papers found the original in his own handwriting, with his many fugitive pieces which he had preserved.

And then, too, the style was so exactly his, when he felt in a humorous mood. We have often said, could it be possible that another could express the same originality of thought and use the same phrases so familiar to us, as Father's!

What my brother Edwin said to your mother, no doubt, was true, but I do not remember the circumstances. I remember my brother Charles took the poem home with him, he was then living in Ohio, and I have an indistinct idea that he intended to have it published, but I am not at all sure on that point, so don't like to assert it as fact.

My father had a fine poetical taste, and wrote a great deal both prose and poetry, but not for publication, but for his own and our amusement; he also had a great taste for drawing and painting. When we were children he used to entertain us

*on winter evenings by getting down the paint box, we seated
around the table, first he would portray something very pathet-
ic, which would melt us to tears, the next thing would be so
comic, that we would be almost wild with laughter. And this
dear good man was your great-great-grandfather.*

*Now my dear give your mama and grandmama my
warmest love*

*Yours very truly
E L Thompson
Elm Cottage & xx xx
March 4th [1879]*

"Family stories being what they are, the fundamental
facts one can get from Babylon Henry is that his father heard
the poem recited a decade and a half before the poem was
published in the Troy Sentinel, and that the original manuscript was seen by the family before it was lost. The letter
reiterated the poem's publication in the Knickerbocker Magazine, but there have been no other stories down any other
family line that confirms that particular magazine," wrote
Mary S. Van Deusen, a present-day Livingston descendent.

The cause was picked up by Jeanne Denig, and her correspondence to William S. Thomas is a trove of Livingston
angst and incredulity:

A few years ago I was much interested in trying to prove that the Night Before Christmas was written by Henry Livingston. I had letters from my mother, your father, & all the others of that generation. All bore testimony to the pleasant tradition & belief that their grandfather had written the verses. But where is the proof?

I hope you will find it! My mother said that her grandfather used the "Dunder & Blitzen" as familiarly as some other people say "Great Scott!" etc etc etc! But alas! It is all hear-say and say-so — no proof.

I was taught to believe that my great grandfather Livingston wrote it. I have taught the same to my children & now my grandchildren believe it.

Pelletreau says it was written in 1822. Grandmother Livingston said she knew the poem before that date. She was born in 1800.

Under the heading "Great grand father's verses," Denig wrote to Thomas on December 25, 1918, from Pittsburgh, Pennsylvania:

My mother was greatly excited when the first edition of the "Night Before Christmas" was published in the name of Clement C. Moore — She bought a copy & brought it to my grandmother, who calmly said "Some one has made a mis-

take – Clement Moore did not write the 'Night Before Christmas.' Your grandfather Henry Livingston wrote it." I was brought up to believe this statement. My grandmother has repeatedly told me all about it– and of having heard it read by Major Henry himself as by himself.

*   *   *

If Guy Livingston has the Livingston family bible, I think there is a poem in that composed by Major Henry on the birth or the death of one of his children. But this is only a "think" on my part. It is vague in the back of my brain.

My grandmother, Eliza Clement Brewer Livingston, knew her father-in-law, Major Henry Livingston, all her life and was on intimate terms with the family from her childhood – she lived with her grandparents Mitchell at "Russ Plass" [the estate adjoining the Livingstons'.] She told me that Major Henry wrote verses all the time, & always at New Year, an address that was published in the Poughkeepsie paper – "Donder & Blitzen" was a familiar expression of his – He wore a night cap in winter & his wife tied her head up in a 'kerchief –

Great grand mother Jane Paterson was very original I have been told. She probably would tie her head up in a 'kerchief if other people wore close night caps – She was quick & lively and did things her own way –

Commodore says "The Night Before Christmas" will ever be a Shakespeare-Bacon sort of affair. He also said the Living-

ston claim should be given publicity – Why not print that a belief exists among the descendants of Henry Livingston that he wrote the verses – start the ball rolling.

Jeanne wrote William again on October 2, 1920:

Of Henry Livingston's actual personal belongings I possess, besides the chessmen, his pair of wine decanters and his engraving of George and Martha Washington and the Curtis children.

We had in this house also his tall clock and the family Bible. The clock, my mother willed to my niece, Mrs. Harold Crosskill, now living in University Heights. She hasn't taken it away & it is still in Sandusky. I was sorry to see it go out of the house, but my brother would have had it, so my mother gave it to his eldest child. The Bible went to my mother's eldest brother & eventually to Guy Livingston now living in Cleveland. He has said that the Bible is to go to my son Robbie. The Bible was in this house until I was quite grown up. I believe that there are some verses in it written by Henry L – upon the death of a child. I have seen them somewhere, and I think they were in the Bible.

I will write Jeannie Gurney. Her mother, (Aunt Susan) was the last of Henry Livingston's children. The Gurney's were burned out two or three times, so much may have been lost. I am sending you to read, the last letter I have in my possession written by Henry Livingston. Please return it. I wish to keep it as it is congratulation upon the birth of my mother's eldest sister [Eliza] who didn't live long. I have a letter written by his wife, our great-grandmother. She was chatty, but neither a good penman nor a good speller. I have heard that she was too full of life & activity to care to bother about such stupid things as spelling and conventional letter writing.

My proof that H.L. wrote the poem is the "say so" of my grandmother Livingston who lived with us until 1878 when she died. She was Eliza Clement Brewer, and lived with her mother & her parents, the Mitchells in the house called "Russ Plass", later bought by Judge Smith Thompson. My grandmother grew up with the Livingston children & was much at Locust Grove. She said that everybody knew that H.L. wrote the poem, & when she was a child she had been invited to spend Christmas with the Livingston children & grandfather had read the poem to them — as his own. My mother said that her father always told or read the poem as having been written by his father. My mother grew up believing it, and taught us to believe it, and grandmother always said "There is no question about it — There has simply been a mistake!"

But with it all, there was no written proof.

Tyron *article,* Christian
Science Monitor, *1920*

Even so, the Livingston claims seemed to gather more momentum, and garnered a more serious inspection by the major press. On August 4, 1920, *The Christian Science Monitor* published a lengthy article in which Winthrop P. Tryon seriously questioned the authorship of the poem, and certainly seemed to find that Livingston had a possible claim. William Sturgis Thomas had supplied Tryon with loads of family correspondence and Henry Livingston's papers to boot, as evidence.

Tryon wrote:

> *To those who like the poems of their childhood well enough to care who wrote them, the seventy-ninth milestone on the Albany Post Road might conceivably be a goal of pilgrimage. For within view of the spot where it is located, lived Henry Livingston Junior, who, according to a tradition handed down through four generations of his descendants and unanimously held by those representing him today, was the author of the famous ballad beginning with the line: 'Twas the night before Christmas, when all through the house.*
>
> *In 1844, a book of poems was published by Moore, and*

the "St. Nicholas" ballad was included in the collection. All but two of the 44 pieces in this book are in iambic meter, and are studiously, elegantly and seriously composed. They are more or less in a moralizing vein, and their style bears some resemblance to that of Whittier. They contain scarcely anything, however, except the ballad, to commend the author as a humorist.

A professor of American literature, whose opinion was recently asked touching the authorship of "The Visit," said that Moore's long possession put the burden of proof on the Livingston claimants; and he remarked that the author, whoever he was, wrote lightly and from the top of his head. Now Livingston did not always write lightly, yet that was his usual way. As for seeking notice or credit for his writings, that he seems regularly to have omitted to do. On one occasion, he went so far as to write a poem for a Poughkeepsie paper as a holiday supplement, or, in the phrase of the times, as a carrier's address, to which he permitted the name of a newsboy, Seth Parsons, to be signed. He was more careful of his fame as an artist than as a writer, for numerous rather crude illustrations, made from drawings of his, are found in the New York Magazine, signed by his first initial and last name, or by his two initials.

In the end, only a little headway had been made. But it was a beginning.

CHAPTER 7

'Twas Only $280,000

I n December 2006, through a private deal, the last remaining handwritten copy of *'Twas the Night Before Christmas* scribbled by Moore's pen was sold for $280,000 to a private collector.

The Associated Press reported on December 19, 2006: "The buyer, identified only as the chief executive officer of a media company, received the copy of the poem this month, just in time to read it to relatives and business associates at a holiday party in his Manhattan apartment, Heritage Auction Galleries president Greg Rohan said."

'Twas the Night Before Christmas
written in Moore's hand

Attendees of the party listened attentively as the new owner read aloud from the frail artifact. They "couldn't believe it," Rohan told the AP. Rohan had personally delivered the poem to its new owner in a protective plastic sleeve. "They thought it was the coolest thing that was," he said. The new owner, Rohan told the press, planned to "keep it forever."

A Visit from St. Nicholas, as it was first titled, gradually became known by its opening line, and morphed into *'Twas the Night Before Christmas*.

From its publication in 1823, the poem became more and more popular, being printed in numerous newspapers around the country. Indeed, it may be the most reprinted poem in in the history of American newspaper publishing and in American letters.

In 1840, William Cullen Bryant, the dean of American poetry

A Visit from Saint Nicholas, *1862*

at the time, included it in his *Selections from the American*

Poets, thus anointing the poem as one of the great contributions to American letters.

T.C. Boyd illustration, 1848

From that point on, its place in American common experience began to grow. in 1848, it was published as a stand-alone book for the first time by Henry M. Onderdonk, illustrated with engravings by Theodore C. Boyd. That book is a collector's item today. It was published for the first time in Canada that same year in the Canadian juvenile series *The Snow Drop, Vol. II, No. 9*, which was also the first time "Merry Christmas" replaced the original "Happy Christmas." About ten years later, the title changed to *The Night Before Christmas* (with lengthy subtitles), when Willis P. Hazard published its standalone version.

In the middle of the Civil War, December 1863, came the first pen and ink drawings of St. Nick by famed illustrator and political cartoonist Thomas Nast, a friend of Mark Twain. About the same time, the first edition to use the title *The Night Before Christmas* by itself, with-

Thomas Nast illustration, 1863

out any subtitles, appeared. It was published by Peter G. Thomson and illustrated by B. Geyser.

One of the most famous editions of the book was published in 1869, when McLoughlin Brothers released a new edition with chromolithographs on every page. Though no illustrator was credited, it was the first full-color edition of the work that was mass-produced.

Visit of St. Nicholas,
McLoughlin Brothers, 1869

The Night Before Christmas had gained a place as part of the national experience. Mark Twain read the poem to his three daughters in their Connecticut mansion, probably from the full-color McLoughlin Brothers edition.

By the 1890s, the poem had gained traction in other countries, with reprints in Britain and Germany.

"Where Santa Claus Lives" by
William H. Partridge (1900)

According to Nancy M. Marshall, there have been more than 1,001 editions of the book. Marshall is a retired Dean of University Libraries at the College of William and Mary. She loves Christmas memorabilia and is the foremost collector of the various editions of A Visit from St. Nicholas, having been at it for more than fifty years. Her lifetime of collecting culminated in her donating her massive and valuable collection to the Special Collections Research Center of William and Mary's Earl Gregg Swem Library. She is also the author of *The Night Before Christmas: A Descriptive Bibliography of Clement Clarke Moore's Immortal Poem*. Wrote Marshall:

"As time passed, it became apparent to me that I would need to devote much more of my time, talent and treasure if I were going to build my collection into the comprehensive one I envisioned. As a result, my collection is now approaching one thousand editions and other items relating to the poem. Gradually, I began to realize that it was, perhaps, one of the largest collections held in private hands, and that someday it would be incumbent upon me to compile a bibliography as my contribution to the scholarly record. This, then, is what you have in hand — a labor of love built upon a lifetime of collecting."

Stereo card, 1888

Various presidents have been huge fans of the book. "My annual Christmas Tree Party for the children at the Women's

Trade Union League Club House in the afternoon seemed to be successful and I left the children eating ice cream and cake very happily," wrote First Lady Eleanor Roosevelt on December 22, 1938. "It was a pleasant experience last night to take part in the program of 'We the People' and to find myself sitting next to Mr. Will Moore, whom we usually see at Warm Springs, Georgia. He read portions from his great-grandfather's poem: 'The Night Before Christmas.' If I had had the time, I would have told him that this is one of the few poems my husband enjoys reading aloud too."

F.D.R. himself, like Bill Clinton, George W. Bush after him, and Barack Obama, all took their turns reading the poem to their own children as well as countless local school-children in various rooms of the White House, as part of the holiday celebrations.

Martin Gardiner, who edited *The Annotated Night Before Christmas*, noted that there more than one hundred spoofs and parodies of the poem, which further indicated how much a part of the American consciousness it had become.

Possibly the most famous was James Thurber's parody, "A Visit from Saint Nicholas (in the Ernest Hemingway Manner)," which appeared in the December 24, 1927 issue of *The New Yorker*. Speaking of New Yorkers, the same magazine's E.B. White started his children's novel *Stuart Little*, about a small mouse in 1945, with the title character's par-

as the great-great-great-great-great granddaughter of Major Henry Livingston Jr.

Foster is a professor of English at Vassar College and, as David Roberts of *Smithsonian Magazine* described him, "a well-known literary gumshoe [who] pioneered the technique of studying the details of a text's wording and syntax to establish authorship, using computerized archives to look for telltale influences. He is best known for identifying Shakespeare as the author of the anonymous poem 'Funeral Elegy' and the journalist Joe Klein as author of the novel 'Primary Colors.'

Mr. Foster has become the Livingston camp's ardent partisan, frequently comparing Mr. Moore in the book to Dr. Seuss's Grinch," wrote *The New York Times* journalist David D. Kirkpatrick in an article about the controversy regarding Moore's authorship.

Burton Rasco,
San Antonio Light

The story had occasionally resurfaced over the years, but no serious investigation had taken place. Burton Rasco had written about the story in *The American Weekly*, but it was much more for amusement, than investigative journalism.

Foster used a mixture of traditional textual scholarship and computer analysis to search and identify unique and unusual usage patterns. Similar techniques had been used before, most notably, to identify the authors of *The Federalist Papers*. Computer forensics alone, however, was not always a sure thing. As Foster himself has pointed out, "The notion has been perpetuated that there's a computer program that can identify authorship, and there isn't."

Mary S. Van Deusen, on the other hand, was no literary scholar. "Mother raised me with the idea that I could write because it was in my genes. She had the same explanation on why I should be able to create art. I fought long and hard against the idea, with a physics major at University of Chicago for the first 3½ years of college, and a career in computer language design." She was accomplished at technical writing as well as video scripts and graphic illustration. "When I took early retirement from IBM Research in 1993, I had no doubt that life would be rich and full. I just never imagined how much so," Van Deusen wrote.

Van Deusen's parents had separated when she was just six weeks old, and her father died when she was eleven. Her penchant for research had not only provided her a career in business, but also spilled into her personal life. First she researched her father (who had published, incidentally, a small volume of poetry himself). Then, around 1995, she became interested in genealogy.

"It seemed that the best way to discover father as a person was to read his poetry. The problem was finding it! Being rather goal-directed, I got into genealogy with the purpose of finding some relative who might have received a book of my father's poetry," she wrote. She tracked down a multitude of ancestors. One of them was Henry Livingston Jr.

"I would never have found Major Henry Livingston if I'd not been searching for Major Bradley Van Deusen. Mother left father when I was 6 weeks old, and all I knew of him was that he was a soldier and a poet, and had died while I was still a child. I was desperate to know him, this man who created half of me, and I thought that in his poetry I'd find HIM. I did have letters father had written begging mother to come back and, in them, he said that he'd burned his manuscripts and the future could do without him. Well, not if his daughter had anything to do about it. But I couldn't find his poems and it seemed as though his future was, indeed, lost. Then I thought that if, perhaps, I took up genealogy, I could find a relative with a book. And that search led me to Henry—another major who was a poet," wrote Van Deusen on her website. "I started out, like you, having no opinion on who actually wrote the poem."

Van Deusen was able to convince Foster to look into the conflict over authorship of the poem. "Talk about watching your life turn left!" she wrote. "My research tendencies are to grab a shovel, check the direction of China and then just keep digging." Foster had retained a healthy skepticism when first presented with the literary case—a bemused literary Sherlock Holmes. But Van Deusen was dogged in her pursuit.

"Mary Van Deusen has always had Christmas spirit to spare. She has been known to keep her tree up until May, and even tells people 'Merry Christmas' in the middle of summer," wrote Samantha Miller in People magazine. With her cherubic face and chatty style, Van Deusen seduced Foster with a very fun challenge.

She had tracked down numerous relatives through her genealogy searches, finding relatives in the Hudson Valley. There she prevailed upon Stephen Livingston Thomas, a 90-something fourth cousin twice removed, asking that he lend her the manuscripts of Henry Livingston Jr. She worked with his fifty-year old son to help locate the now hidden manuscripts. It was the father who had carried the torch of Henry's authorship for more than twenty years, but who had failed in his own eyes, and those of the literary world, to significantly change opinion on the subject. Mary explained the possible involvement of Foster, and the papers were handed over. She was a juggernaut.

Together Foster and Van Deusen went to Clinton House,

the local historical society for Dutchess County. Once the two local historians were told of the mission these two were on, both Mrs. Eileen Hayden and Mrs. Bernice Thomas opined without hesitation and with absolute authority: "That poem was written by Major Henry Livingston Junior," Foster recalled.

Working diligently, the indefatigable Van Deusen and the sleuthing Foster found numerous other poems, originally anonymously published, that had heretofore not been attributed to Livingston but that were, without a doubt, the Major's work. But even by Foster's own admission, they never found a copy of the *Night Before Christmas* poem in Livingston's handwriting of any kind. No "smoking gun," as he once stated. He then turned to Moore.

"In textual analysis, the author of a Questioned Document may be identified by what's been taken—vocabulary, phrasing, and metaphor lifted from other writers. As it happens, Clement Clarke Moore was a learned man but not terribly original," Foster wrote. "Plunk a finger down almost anywhere in his book of 'Poems.' Select a phrase that describes nature—'clouds of darker hue,' 'diamond raindrops,' 'summer's balmy breath,' 'rustling foliage,' 'verdant islets,' 'yielding sand,'" wrote Foster. Many of the phrases in the first poems in Moore's book were, according to Foster, lifted from the works of the English poet Robert Southey

(1774-1843). Other phrases, Foster maintained, were taken straight from the poet Bernard Barton (1784-1849), and still others from the American Timothy Dwight's "Conquest of Canaan," published in 1785.

"The professor's verse is highly derivative, — so much so that his reading can be tracked, and his poems dated, by the dozens of phrases borrowed and recycled by his sticky fingered muse," wrote Foster. "It would be unfair to call Moore's extensive borrowing plagiarism. Poetry has less to do with original creation than with reassembling familiar language into something new." Still, Moore's style was set. He emulated, in his own writing, whatever he was reading at the time.

A Visit from St. Nicholas was an anapestic poem; a specific cadence was required. The two most popular versions of this type of poetry were, according to Foster, Christopher Anstey's "New Bath Guide" and William King's "The Toast to An Heroick Poem." As Foster pointed out, these were slightly subversive poems, and Moore probably read them to stay abreast of the newest literature, no matter how unseemly or profane. But it would be highly unlikely he would have considered these sing-songy poems as something suitable for his children to read.

David D. Kirkpatrick, writing about Foster's findings in *The New York Times*, relayed that "[o]ne of King's poems, for example, described a hung-over Apollo struggling to pilot his chariot across the sky. Among other details, Apollo's 'coursers' 'prance' like Santa's reindeer. 'A Visit' borrows its meter, style, images and vocabulary from both poets and a few others in the same vein, Mr. Foster writes. But Moore wrote only one undisputed anapestic poem, 'The Pig and the Rooster,' moralizing about laziness and arrogance. It borrows almost nothing from the poems that influenced the author of 'A Visit.' Moore generally mimicked pious poets, Mr. Foster said. Henry Livingston, however, lifted frequently from such bawdy anapests, by Mr. Foster's analysis. Livingston wrote anapestic verses to his family every Christmas. Many of them borrow language and form from King and Anstey, and so resemble 'A Visit.'"

Foster cited numerous other points. Moore never wished anyone a Merry Christmas in writing. Further, "A Visit from St. Nicholas" stuck out like a sore thumb in Moore's book of "Poems." Moore also changed the names of the reindeer to more English names, while Livingston was brought up reading and speaking Dutch as well as English.

More than anything else, Foster found Moore's own detective work, in 1844, before including "A Visit" in his own book of "Poems," odd. As others have also pointed out, Moore claimed to have made only "two changes" to the poem when he included it in his volume. But there are more than fifty changes from the original poem to his 1844 version. It seems clear that Moore made those changes based on the 1830 printed broadside that the former publisher of the *Troy Sentinel* supplied, in which a number of those changes had already been made by subsequent newspaper editors over the years.

Foster also cited the merino sheep book with its odd dedication, and where Moore apparently took credit for translating the work (or was it incorrectly attributed to Moore?) for he clearly had not translated the work, given that the true translator/author's name was in the back of the book, with the copyright notice.

He further pointed out that Moore was not above literary chicanery in his quest for poetic fame. As a young poet, he had published his poems anonymously with the initial —L. attached to them. Probably as a reaction to the lack of coverage of his book, or pique over the tepid reviews, there appears a review in The Churchman, the magazine of the Protestant Episcopal Church. It "gave Moore a ringing endorsement, a review suitable for framing," wrote Foster. "I don't know for sure who wrote it but the author of that flattering Churchman blurb signs himself 'L.' Perhaps the old Professor wasn't humorless after all. Perhaps he even wrote his own book review."

Foster published his version of the sleuthing in a book

titled *Author Unknown: Tales of a Literary Detective*, published in 2000 by Henry Holt & Co. Foster's finding for Livingston captivated the literary world. News of Foster's findings appeared in *The New York Times*, *The Boston Globe*, *The Washington Post*, the *Chicago Tribune*, the *San Francisco Chronicle*, and the *Los Angeles Times*. *The New York Times* ran the headline, "Literary Sleuth Casts Doubt on the Authorship of an Iconic Christmas Poem." In the ensuing article, its author, David D. Kirkpatrick, wrote:

"'A Visit' is a hodgepodge of Livingston's favorite images, Mr. Foster writes. Livingston's light poems are crowded with flying children, animals, fairies, boats and other vehicles, like Santa's flying sleigh and reindeer. Livingston also fancied himself an expert on the Arctic and wrote elsewhere of Lapland's reindeer. He also wrote of the Norse god Thor, whose chariot was pulled by flying goats. Livingston would have been familiar with the Dutch legend of annual visits from St. Nicholas. The original author of the poem also sprinkled extraneous exclamation points through Santa's reindeer roll call, another Livingston habit. 'It is vintage Livingston,' Mr. Foster said."

Kirkpatrick continued: "In other Christmas poems [Moore] admonished his own children to be humble, mindful of their mortality and aloof from transient pleasures. He condemned 'immodest verse' with 'no other recommendations than the glow of its expressions and the tinkling of its syllables, or the wanton allurement of the ideas that it conveys.' The poem's St. Nicholas enjoys a pipe, but Mr. Moore railed against tobacco as 'opium's treacherous aid.'"

"The real issue was always, would a man of God, a bible professor, tell a lie?" Mr. Foster said to Kirkpatrick in his interview. "No one was willing to say, yeah, he would. But he did."

The mystery had been solved!

Or had it?

CHAPTER 9

Backlash!

The very nature of being in the debunking business is that you are bound to offend or just flat out piss someone off. While the press feted Foster and his findings, a storm of rebuttal was gathering. Most notable among those bothered by Foster's suppositions was Stephen Nissenbaum.

In addition to his previously cited credentials, Nissenbaum was a professor at the University of Massachusetts at Amherst and the co-author of *Salem Possessed: The Social Origins of Witchcraft*, which was recognized as "a landmark in early American studies."

Nissenbaum rejoined Foster's case in the academic journal *Common-Place*, in an article titled, "There Arose Such a
Clatter: Who Really Wrote 'The Night Before Christmas'?
(And Why Does It Matter?)." Nissenbaum came at the controversy well informed, as he had written his own history of
the holiday season in *The Battle for Christmas*, which Knopf
first published in 1996. Without saying it outright, it was apparent that Nissenbaum thought Foster had painted Moore
with a tarred brush. Nissenbaum was happy to come to a
fellow Columbia alumnus' aid.

"Foster's textual evidence is ingenious, and his essay is
as entertaining as a lively lawyer's argument to the jury. If he
had limited himself to offering textual evidence about sim-
ilarities between "The Night Before Christmas' and poems
known to have been written by Livingston, he might have
made a provocative case for reconsidering the authorship of
America's most beloved poem—a poem that helped create
the modern American Christmas," wrote Nissenbaum.

Nissenbaum argued that Foster had gone too far. Foster's
use of "textual analysis, in tandem with biographical data,
proves that Clement Clarke Moore could not have written"
the famous poem. In the words of an article on Foster's the-
ory that appeared in the *New York Times*, 'He marshals a battery of circumstantial evidence to conclude that the poem's

spirit and style are starkly at odds with the body of Moore's other writings.' With that evidence and that conclusion I take strenuous exception," continued Nissenbaum.

"Moore was neither the dull pedant nor the joy-hating prude," wrote Nissenbaum. "It is clear enough that [Livingston] and Moore, whatever their political and even temperamental differences, were both members of the same patrician social class, and that the two men shared a fundamental cultural sensibility that comes through in the verses they produced. If anything, Livingston, born in 1746, was more a comfortable gentleman of the high eighteenth century, whereas Moore, born thirty-three years later in the midst of the American Revolution, and to loyalist parents at that, was marked from the beginning with a problem in coming to terms with the facts of life in republican America."

Nissenbaum discredited the autograph that Foster ascribed to Moore in the merino sheep book, positing that another person had penciled in the name, and that Moore himself was not in the habit of adding his "A.M.," which signals a scholar's master's degree.

"The charge will not stick," pronounced Nissenbaum. "It is clear even to my own inexpert eye that the penned inscription...is not written in Moore's rather distinctive hand."

Nissenbaum argued that if Moore was as prudish and conservative as Foster painted him, and if he was so afraid of how its frivolity would reflect badly on him, why, then, did Moore not object publicly to having his name attached to it by Charles Fenno Hoffman in 1837, and why did he claim the poem again in 1844? And if he was as pious as Foster countered, then why would he claim something that was not his?

Nissenbaum maintained that Moore, and not Livingston, was the author of A Visit. Nissenbaum then posed the final question: Did Moore in fact actually write "The Night Before Christmas?" Nissenbaum aped the vocabulary of a prosecuting attorney, aping Foster's lawyerly conclusion. He felt Moore did in fact have the "means, the opportunity, and even the motive to write the poem. Like Don Foster's, my evidence must necessarily be circumstantial, but I believe mine is better than his. Some of my evidence is quite straightforward. All of it is based on the belief that historical circumstance helped make Clement Moore a figure of greater complexity than either his admirers or his detractors have recognized...."

CHAPTER 10

Triumph of a Kind

On December 3, 2011, *The Boston Globe* heralded the publishing of an important first. Under the headline "A Clatter of Claims to a Classic: Maine publisher champions rival author of old favorite" came this newsflash:

"A new edition of the poem popularly known as 'The Night Before Christmas' is being published next week by a small press in Freeport, Maine. Handsomely illustrated, it will sell for $150 and make a thoughtful, if not inexpensive, holiday gift," reported Joseph P. Kahn. "The new edition of 'The Night Before Christmas' is credited to Henry Livingston Jr. It also makes a statement. The book credits authorship to farmer-poet Henry Livingston Jr., not Clement Clarke Moore, the man widely celebrated as the poem's creator. And therein lies a literary whodunit with more loose ends than Santa Claus has whiskers."

An Account of a Visit From St. Nicholas, *Kahn Publishers, 2011*

Kahn made reference to *Author Unknown*, writing, "Foster's book touched off a flurry of stories questioning whether one of the most familiar poems in the English language was written by the man who said he wrote it. Foster has since backed off from taking sides, however, calling it one mystery that won't ever be cleared up, or need to be."

"'It's an old controversy that never has been, nor shall be, resolved to everyone's satisfaction,'" says Foster," Kahn reported. "In literary studies, we often say the text itself is more important than the author. And nowhere is this more true than with this poem."

St. Nicholas Press published the book as a limited edition. Founder Michael Billmeyer considered it a chance, as Kahn said, "to right a longstanding case of mistaken poetic identity."

Even the Poetry Foundation got into the act, reprinting the *Globe* piece and reminding readers of the poem's success and importance in the American literary canon.

Other scholars and experts also chimed in. Seth Kaller was one of the most vociferous. Seth Kaller was born into the collecting and authenticating business. For generations Kaller's family has been renowned in the rarified world of rare stamp and coin collecting. Seth became world famous for owning a complete block of the famous/infamous upside down Jenny Curtis airplane stamps. By the late 1980s, Kaller started to steer his family's operations into the world of acquiring, authenticating and appraising memorabilia and rare American documents such as the personal correspondence of U.S. presidents and other prominent Americans. He is among the most famous authenticators in North America.

Kaller is the largest dealer in historic documents and has an excellent reputation for his eye and his authentication. He has worked with some of the leading institutions in America, including the Smithsonian, the National Constitution Center, the Gettysburg National Civil War Museum, the New York Stock Exchange, Mount Vernon, the University of Virginia, Rice University, Yale University, Kennedy Space Center, the Lincoln Museum, several presidential libraries, and national parks museums.

Kaller has been a staunch advocate of the Moore camp, and has used his website to make his case:

"When the 83-year-old Moore penned The New-York Historical Society copy, he explained that he had originally composed the verse for his two daughters, using a 'portly, rubicund Dutchman' in the neighborhood as his model for St. Nicholas (New-York Historical Society Quarterly Bulletin, January 1919, 111 and 114). Every piece of documentary evidence supports Moore's authorship.

"Many years later, descendants of Henry Livingston, Jr. mistakenly convinced themselves that their patriarch was 'the real' author based on their memory of his reading a Christmas poem to the family. Their 'evidence' was discredited time and again, so the family narrative continued to evolve."

Kaller has also made his case in an essay he wrote for the Winter 2004 issue of the New-York Journal of American History, titled "The Moore Things Change."

Like Nissenbaum, Kaller discredited Foster for the inaccurate accusation that Moore signed the merino sheep book, thus taking credit for the translation. He also chided Foster, as did Nissenbaum, for painting such a prudish portrait of Moore. He claimed that Moore was no more a Scrooge than anyone else, especially with all the children in his house. And he discredited the linguistics that Foster cited showing that the words and speech patterns in *A Visit* were inconsistent with the body of Moore's poetry.

Kaller made some excellent points, but his championing of Moore seemed to verge on hagiographic. He claimed that Moore had "been unjustly accused of taking false credit for the classic holiday poem. But any unbiased look at the evidence — documentary, historical and linguistic — must lead to the conclusion that Moore was indeed the work's author...."

He continued: "I started this investigation with a willingness to let the chips fall where they may. In the end, I can conclude that when all the 'personal opinions' and 'personal rhetoric' are put aside, there is not a shred of real evidence to support the Henry Livingston case. He may have been a great guy, and he may have even written a Christmas poem, long forgotten, but he didn't write this one."

Kaller had used a team of researchers, whom he had at his disposal, and he was not alone in this opinion. Vernon Benjamin, the impeccable historian who penned the two-volume edition of *The History of the Hudson River Valley*, agreed with Kaller and Nissenbaum. While he was a fan of the Livingstons, he saw no reason to award the poem to Henry.

Another Foster dissenter was Scott Norsworthy, the "Melvilliana" blogger who has established himself as one of the foremost authorities in the United States on Herman Melville, and who also has an affinity for *A Visit*, or Moore, or both. A dogged, indefatigable researcher, he proved a worthy adversary and capable scholar, who regardless of whether you agreed with him or not had found some of the most amazing tidbits in the search for this truth.

Time and again, he dug up obscure reprints of the poems from far-flung newspapers, from the early and mid-1800s, via data searches and using internet tools. He also unearthed minute but important sideline correspondence from various newspapers of the day. As he accumulated more evidence, it was clear he, too, found against Foster.

In the piece he wrote, Norsworthy praised Kallci for writing that Nissenbaum "expertly confirms in his January 2001 essay at Common Place, [how] Don Foster woefully misrepresented the character and abilities of Clement C. Moore. Foster's mudslinging...carried plenty of argumentative weight, or tried to: it's easier for readers to deprive Moore of due credit for authorship of the classic Christmas poem when he's made to resemble a nasty combination of Scrooge and Grinch."

Norsworthy chides Foster for, in one instance, incorrectly vilifying Moore. Foster had erroneously chastised Moore for challenging a young seminarian during the 1844 Christmas season, one Joseph Newton Wattson.

Wattson had jokingly said to a fellow seminarian, ""Don't you know, Prescott, that there is a number of Jesuit students in disguise here at the General, and that when they have made all the converts they can, they are going openly to Rome themselves?"" The listener took the joke in earnest, and in a time when fears were rampant (the seminary had experienced two recent and public controversies, and of course Irish immigration in the city was increasing and worries of Papist overrun were high), the seminary held an inquiry. Students were accused of conspiracy against the church. These were serious accusations. Moore was the secretary who recorded the minutes, and later had to send out the correspondence noting that the students had been accused. Years later, a former seminarian of that class, Clarence Augustus Walworth, would attempt to set the record straight, and explain that Moore, despite whatever impressions people may have had of him at the time, was in fact a moderating influence during this small but serious crisis.

Norsworthy, in his admirable way, had uncovered an obscure Ecclesiastical book by Walworth, a classmate of Joseph Newton Wattson. Ironically, Walworth eventually dropped out of the Theological Seminary, converted to Catholicism and became a priest. He retold the story in his memoir *The Oxford Movement* in America. Walworth wrote of Moore:

Santa Claus himself could not be more welcome to chil-
dren than was this odd and genial man upon his appearance
in the Hebrew class. He was very particular in his ways; but
one great feature of his peculiarity was, that he was utterly un-
artificial. He was droll, but unconsciously so. He never joked
in the class, but always something made the classroom seem
merry when he was in it. He was a true scholar in Hebrew.
His knowledge of Hebrew words did not seem to be derived
from the dictionary alone. He knew each word familiarly, and
remembered all the different places where it occurred in the
Hebrew Bible, and so could prove its significance in one place
by the meaning which necessarily attached to it elsewhere.

Foster had created a stir with his dramatic flair. But in
painting an unflattering portrait of the well liked, if pious
Moore, he had somehow awoken a loyal cadre of acolytes.

There is no question reading it some fifteen years
later that Foster's points come across like a prosecutor
making his argument. As in any good trial, Foster had
scored some hits and had made some mistakes; the defense,
waiting patiently, pounced on those and used them to
discredit him. Regardless, a blow had been struck against
Moore and for Livingston, even with the detractions,
some of which were notable.

Also, although the Moore camp countered with excellent

scholarly erudition, they themselves made far-flung state-
ments and emphatic claims that were clearly not provable,
and that were seemingly more emotional than simple fact.

There was still more to come.

CHAPTER 11

Enter MacDonald P. Jackson

Not long after Mary Van Deusen enlisted the help of Donald Foster, she was also approached by another famous linguistic expert, MacDonald P. Jackson. This was the equivalent of inviting a major heavyweight champion to a local prizefight.

Like Foster before him, Jackson possesses impeccable, almost unassailable, internationally recognized credentials. A New Zealand scholar of English literature, MacDonald curried worldwide accolades for his assiduous investigations into Shakespeare's texts and, like Foster, specializes in questions of authorship. In 1964, MacDonald achieved his B. Litt after he finished his studies at Merton College, Oxford. Among his many fellowships have been one from the Folger Shakespeare Library and another from the Huntington Library. In addition, Jackson is an anthologist, literary historian, and contributor to the *Oxford History of New Zealand Literature in English*.

"My interest in the authorship of 'A Night Before Christmas' was first aroused by a chapter on the subject in Donald Foster's book," wrote Jackson in his book, *Who Wrote "The Night Before Christmas"?* "But skeptical rejoinders to Foster's case by Joe Nickell, Seth Kaller, Stephen Nissenbaum, and others soon alerted me to the complexities of the authorship problem.

"When in 2011 I became interested in debates about the authorship of 'The Night Before Christmas.' I could read the texts of Clement Clarke Moore's POEMS (1844) through the electronic database Literature Online..., while poems by Henry Livingston were available on Mary Van Deusen's website devoted to him," Jackson continued. "In December of that year I emailed Mary to ask a few questions. Before long she established a 'Research Site' that provided me with ever increasing information."

Jackson spent more than a year examining the question of authorship regarding *A Visit from St. Nicholas*. He and a

host of other academics applied modern computational sty-
listics techniques to the corpora of verse left by both claimants, including a new test: statistical analysis of phonemes.

Jackson didn't join the fray until late 2016. All the par-
ticipants eagerly awaited his entrance. He corresponded
with Norsworthy at "Melvilliana," writing in October 2016,
"readers will find all pro-Moore points duly considered
in my book....It is true that stylistic evidence for Henry Livingston's authorship of the poem must be weighed against
the documentary evidence for Moore's. This is what I attempt
to do. The case for Livingston is by no means based sole-
ly on stylo-statistical data. My conclusion is that Livingston must have been the true author of the poem, as his
descendants claim."

Norsworthy subsequently reviewed Jackson's book on
Amazon. He maintained that Jackson was out of his depth,
as he was not an *American* literary scholar, but "I hope his
method will succeed in getting the writers right....I'm ridicu-
lously glad to allow plenty of theoretical room for the merits
of using internal textual evidence to establish authorship.
With better analytics, maybe function words and phonemes
will prove useful outside of early modern drama. If so, by all
means let's crunch the numbers 'til Christmas!"

Norsworthy went on to scoff at Jackson's effort, discred-
iting Jackson's points and rebutting with his own counter

arguments, without fully presenting Jackson's. He summarized Jackson's points with some frivolity (shocking for him, actually), writing, "By my calculations, the real probability that Clement C. Moore wrote 'The Night Before Christmas' is still right around 102%, give or take a couple of percentage points. Fortunately, however, Professor Jackson has the scruples of a first-rate scholar. He makes his errant way so earnestly that it's easy to spot the wrong turns."

Norsworthy noted Jackson's "false premises" and "[d]isregard of historical and biographical evidence" as placing his faith in "over confidence in numbers," referring to the computer calculations Jackson used to compare the two writers' styles in their poems. He then accused Jackson of having a tin ear. It was not a review; in essence, it was a rebuttal.

Jackson's book, however, is in truth evenhanded and erudite. Where Foster has a flair for the dramatic, making sweeping accusations and misstepping here and there, Jackson's book is very careful, and sometimes plodding, but extremely thorough. Despite Norsworthy's dismissal, the book does in fact score a lot of good hits. But, alas, it is a fool's errand, as Foster found out before him.

In the end, it came back to this: How many angels can sit on the head of a pin? Or, how many literary professors does it take to screw in a light bulb? The question starts out like a fun parlor game, or better yet, a good literary quest, and ends up with a lot of accomplished men and women name-calling one another. One wonders what became of the holiday spirit that the poem supposedly invokes.

The only evidence that will ever satisfy both sides is an original copy, dated before the publication, in either man's hand...or in someone else's. Short of that, this issue will belong up there with the great philosophical questions of the time, no matter what either side says. It's all conjecture, both sides, no matter how much they stamp their feet and tell you they are right.

And so the enlightened had engaged in an inconclusive battle, which had stalemated. It was now the public's turn to take up the question, adopting a more democratic view on the subject. They would have their say... *and* their day in court.

CHAPTER 12

The Trial

Troy is very proud of its place in history in having published this great poem. On the building that was the former home of the editorial offices of the *Troy Sentinel* is a bronze plaque commemorating the event.

On Wednesday night, December 18, 2013, the Rensselaer County Courthouse was packed to the rafters with the most boisterous courtroom that fine old establishment ever had to suffer. Before the bustling courtroom benches, two of the most prominent lawyers in Troy, New York, argued

Plaque on former Troy Sentinel building

before retired State Supreme Court Judge Bud Malone. Crowd attendance was estimated to be more than 500 people, there to attend the holiday spectacle.

"For one night, the legalese and gravity of cases that typically inhabit this ornate courthouse...were set aside. Casey, Malone, attorney E. Stewart Jones and a cast of daffy witnesses in period costume turned this house of the law into a playful theater for 'Livingston v. Moore: Who Really Wrote "A Visit from St. Nicholas"?'" reported a gleeful *Times-Union*.

Real court officers, a court clerk, and a court stenographer gave the proceedings an authentic court room experience, but the spirit of the event was fun and lively.

"The lawyers took sides: Jones for long-accepted author Clement Clarke Moore; Casey for Henry Livingston Jr., whose descendants claim he actually

Poster for The Trial Before Christmas

wrote the poem for which Moore took credit," wrote Bryan Fitzgerald in the *Times-Union of Albany*. "Jones and Casey shed their courthouse manners, taking potshots at each other, the court, the city and its politics. When Casey called the ghost of Livingston to the witness stand, Jones objected, saying dead people should not be allowed to testify. Casey's rebuttal: "If they can vote in Troy, they can testify in Troy."

The Trial Before Christmas at the Troy Courthouse

The mock trial featured all kinds of chicanery and good cheer. "Rensselaer County Historian Kathryn Sheehan and actors portraying Moore and Livingston all testified. The resurrected witnesses came out from a door behind the bench through a thick plume of smoke, lime-green light and thunderous applause. The jury of six was chosen by whoever had a red 'J' inside their programs. A saxophone-toting Santa serenaded the court as the panel deliberated after an hour and 40 minutes of testimony and argument," continued Fitzgerald.

Jones joked that Casey and his legal team, which included his daughter Molly, were taking the event too seriously, when he pointed to Casey's red holiday socks.

At the end of the trial, the jury deliberated and came to a conclusion, which was handed to the venerable bench dignitary Malone.

"Ladies and gentlemen, we have a hung jury!" bellowed the judge. The crowd roared with laughter; boos, hisses, and guffaws echoed through the chambers.

Casey requested a retrial the following year. The crowd cheered.

And indeed, during the Troy Victorian Stroll on December 7, 2014, a retrial took place, organized by the same man, Duncan Crary, who had created the previous year's festivities. The same two lawyers and the same judge reconvened a year later. The trial was full of fun and frivolity, wrote Michael DeMasi in the *Albany Business Review*, which "included a high-

Attorney E. Stewart Jones makes his argument during the trial

powered lawyer wearing mistletoe-and-holly pants openly cozying up to the judge (a fellow Albany Law School alum); another lawyer reciting verses from Robert Frost, Geoffrey Chaucer and Bob Dylan; well-timed one-liners and zingers; testimony from three ghosts; sleigh bells ringing; and even a visit from Elvis."

This time, a trial jury of two men and four women reached a verdict. They found for the plaintiff, Henry Livingston Jr. Cheers, boos, and laughter once again roared through the crowd.

The event was playful and enjoyable and a good time was had by all, a reminder that the holiday season, and the poem, were more about those things, regardless of who had written it.

CHAPTER 13

Conclusion

FACT: No copy of the poem exists in either man's hand that pre-dates the original publication of the poem in 1823.

FACT: The 1825 handwritten copy of *A Visit* by Maryl Odell was written in her hand. There is no evidence whatsoever that it came from Moore or his family. It was found, along with some other Moore poems, among the Odell family papers. End of this particular story.

FACT: The stories connecting Moore and the *Troy Sentinel* via any of the local inhabitants are not fact, they are speculation—no one knows for sure. Someone obviously gave the poem to Holley. But there is no documented evidence that Moore or any relative or friend, including Sackett or Butler, ever took the poem and handed it to the paper. How the poem came to the paper, and anonymously, no one knows. Even Holley and Tuttle could only surmise. Memory was foggy.

FACT: Moore almost always signed his poems — L., and Livingston almost always signed his poems — R. for publication. But not always. *A Visit from St. Nicholas* was left with no attribution.

FACT: Neither man ever published any of his other works with the *Troy Sentinel* before or after.

FACT: No connection between Livingston and the *Troy Sentinel* has ever been proved.

FACT: The earliest extant handwritten copy of *A Visit* in Moore's own hand is from 1853, nine years after its original publication.

FACT: The earliest copy of *A Visit* in Moore's own papers was the broadsheet from 1830 printed by the *Troy Sentinel*, which Tuttle sent to Moore before the publication of *Poems*. The poem reprinted in that book makes changes from that broadsheet, not from the original published poem.

FACT: Moore told several people he made few editorial changes to the poem. But in fact, there were 55 editorial changes from the 1823 published poem to the 1830 broad sheet. And the version published in *Poems* had another 14 changes from the broadsheet.

FACT: Livingston signed several correspondences with the phrase "Happy Christmas"; Moore never did that we know of.

FACT: Livingston spoke and read Dutch. Moore was a language professor, but his areas of expertise were Hebrew, Greek, and Latin. Yes, he did translations from other languages, but he was not fluent in any of them, and certainly not Dutch.

FACT: Two world-acknowledged experts confirmed that the language of the poem, as analyzed by sophisticated computer programs, is more in keeping with Livingston than

Moore. It is not proof. At the same time, it must be taken into consideration. It may have flaws, but no person who has performed this test has suggested any other outcome.

FACT: There is no evidence that Moore ever claimed authorship of A Visit even after it had been ascribed to him in 1837 in Charles Fenno Hoffman's poetry collection. He neither claimed it, nor disowned it. No correspondence of any kind addresses it at all.

FACT: Moore claimed authorship of A Visit only after he asked Tuttle how he came by the poem and received an answer, along with a copy of the broadsheet.

FACT: Moore, in 1844, never gave a head note to his—and possibly the country's—most famous poem, even though he gave lengthy head notes, or summaries, to other, much lesser verses.

FACT: Livingston never claimed authorship of the poem in his lifetime.

FACT: Both men loved their children and were well-loved, well-remembered fathers.

FACT: "A Visit From St. Nicholas" or "The Night Before Christmas" (whichever you prefer) remains the most reprinted poem ever written by an American, and is easily the most famous poem in the American literary canon.

FACT: Both camps have set up incredible and extensive research vehicles for both authors. We know more about each of these fine men than has ever been known or discovered before. Regardless of your own conclusions, research in the field has increased our overall knowledge of them and their times.

CHAPTER 14

Reason

U nlike his great-great-great-great-grandfather, and his father's father, Clement C. Moore II did not go to Columbia. He went to Princeton. He is not a Latin, Greek, or ecumenical scholar. He is not a minister. But, like the men who preceded him, he is very much at the center of his community's heart. Clement C. Moore II is a longtime business executive and a partner in several firms. Since 1986 he has been President of Kenwood Galloria, Inc. and has been Managing Partner of Mariemont Holdings, LLC since 1980. He is a Trustee of 5 CRM Funds and Wt

Investment Trust I since October 1999. He is a trustee of The Morgan Library & Museum. Originally the private library of financier Pierpont Morgan (1837-1913), it contains one of the world's most valuable collections of books, manuscripts, and papers. He has been a trustee of a number of smaller museums up and down the East Coast, from Maryland to Connecticut. He is a collector of Rembrandt drawings and other art, which he has gifted to Harvard, Princeton, and other small museums. He has been a contributor to the Metropolitan Museum of Art and the New York Botanical Garden.

The Livingston family remains as large and successful as ever. Their dozens of family mansions are still some of the most coveted private homes in the Hudson Valley. As late as 1998 Bob Livingston, who hailed from the South at the time, became Speaker of the House of Representatives after controlling the powerful House Appropriations Committee. The famed Clermont manse has played host to many of the Livingston family reunions that take place every five years. While there are now Livingstons all around the world who are direct descendants of this family, there are others who are still involved in local politics, and who serve on public and private boards. Their power and influence still steer the valley today.

People like answers. Mysteries are popular because at the

end, the author ties up the questions at hand in a neat little bow and hands it off to the reader. A literary bon-bon of sorts. No such wrapping up is available here. To say one has drawn his or her own conclusion is fine. For anyone to claim it as fact is incorrect.

Only a copy of the poem, in one man's hand or the other's, will satisfy this question. This of course probably will never happen.

"It's an old controversy that never has been, nor shall be, resolved to everyone's satisfaction," said Don Foster, years after the publication of his (controversial) book.

If you are a fan of Clement C. Moore and his camp, you may rejoice. Millions and millions of copies of this poem have borne his name for more than one hundred seventy-five years, through two centuries, and now into a third.

Few publishers would be willing, on an academic's hunch, to put Livingston's name on the book at this point, unless the publisher had a built-in audience or sale. With today's discoverability, and with the online presence so big, to use Livingston's name on the cover instead of Moore's would be tantamount to consigning the project to publishing hell. Many uninformed consumers would think they may have gotten the wrong book. Practicality wins the conversation. Only one book bears both men's names on Amazon.com. Even the one that bore only

Henry's name was a small, limited printing.

Either man may have rightly written it. We will never know for sure. But what matter if one did and one did not? Do the meanings of the lines change? Does it make it more or less valuable in some way? Does it change the fact that the poem has been held dear by generations and generations of people around the world? Do I think less of Moore or Livingston for not having written it? It is remotely possible that neither man wrote it. Then what?

In the end, I am very fond of Clement C. Moore II, the distant relative of Moore himself, who, when asked a few years ago his thoughts on the controversy, replied to *The New York Times*, "It is the poem itself that is important, not the authorship."

Mysteries aside, I happen to agree.

Epilogue

Every year *The Night Before Christmas* (as *A Visit* has come to be known) tops the bestseller list in one edition or another. Hundreds and hundreds of thousands of the various books are sold in all its forms. In 2016 alone, according to Nielsen BookScan, more than half a million units of all the different editions were sold. More important, many of those editions were placed in the hands of children who would hear for the first time the magic and jingle of the opening lines, and be whisked into the magical world of the poem, just as generations before had.

And every year the poem is read. It has been read aloud by presidents and first ladies. Movie stars and great actors. It has been read at Trinity Church and St. Luke's of the Field. It has been read at Clermont, the historic manse of the Livingstons.

Clement C. Moore grave vigil

For more than 100 years, a ritual has taken place at the Church of the Intercession, the house of worship that shares the grounds with Trinity Cemetery in Washington Heights. "The tradition was apparently initiated by a vicar at the chapel named Milo Hudson Gates," reports Bower Boys: New York City History.

"Hundreds of children, carrying lanterns and torches in the old days, gathered around Moore's gravestone and sang Christmas songs. 'Carols were sung and wreaths placed on the grave,' according to a 1919 report. The famous poem by Moore was then recited... This tradition has survived into modern day with some interesting variations. Frequently a person dressed as Saint Nicholas (the saint, not the Santa) leads the procession. In recent decades, a person of some renown reads the poem..."

The book has also been read aloud at Locust Grove, at the Samuel F.B. Morse mansion (the original Livingston House no longer exists), during the holidays to commemorate the season and as a tribute to Livingston.

Samuel F.B. Morse mansion at Locust Grove

More importantly, the poem has been read in the living rooms and dens, and at the bedsides of children all over the world. Generation after generation of children have gone to bed, as John T. Parker said more than 100 years ago, with one eye open, waiting to hear the prancing and pawing of each little hoof, and the hearty ho-ho-ho of Santa Claus.

Recently, my family and I were cleaning out a number of musty old boxes in our attic and happened on some dusty old VHS tapes. They needed to be thrown away. But I was curious as to what was on them. I fed tape after tape into an old VHS player that still worked (miracle of miracles) to make sure nothing of value, especially sentimental value, was being discarded. A blank one here. An old televised sporting event there. Snippets of a television special or old movie.

Then one I popped in stopped me dead in my tracks. It was a Christmas from when my two sons were four years old. It was, I am sad to say, many, many years ago. Our old dogs were suddenly alive again, a white German Shepherd and a German Shorthaired Pointer. They milled through shot after shot, tails wagging, tongues hanging out, faces happy. The crinkle of the discarded Christmas wrapping

My sons Dylan and Dawson with Santa. The circle is complete.

paper under their paws. The living room, now three houses ago, suddenly lit warmly by the glow of our Christmas tree. My father, alive again, his big laugh filling the room.

And there on the sofa were my two little sons, still flush with the euphoria of having received their Christmas presents. X-men. Hot Wheels. And then, as the tape rolled on, I opened the book, and the immortal lines began. "'Twas the night before Christmas..." The boys smiled and settled in. I wish I could tell you how raptly they listened, but that would be a lie. They listened for a bit. Then got bored and wanted to play with their toys. They poked one another. They twisted and squirmed.

Memories came flooding back, and I remembered feeling slightly discouraged that the kids were being, well, kids. As we neared the end of the poem, I remembered relief suddenly being in sight. It all seemed so forced and silly, suddenly, me trying to impose this thing on them.

But then, when at long last I got to the last line, lo and behold, they chimed in with me, gleefully, "Merry Christmas to all! And to all a good night!"

And I smiled.

"Happy Christmas to all, and to all a good night!"

Acknowledgments

Any author of such an effort owes a great debt of gratitude to those who went before him. Firstly, I remain in awe of both Clement C. Moore and Henry Livingston Jr., both of whom were very accomplished men. And also to recognize the special place in American literary history these two men hold—Orville L. Holley and Norman Tuttle. Next would be Washington Irving whose influence on Christmas traditions extends even to today.

During the course of my inquiry, I poured over more than 500 original sources, including letters, interviews, and articles, from various websites and research libraries. Special thanks and appreciation for their work and scholarship would be to Mary Van Deusen, Donald Foster, Seth Keller, Karl Felsen, Stephen Nissenbaum, Scott Norsworthy, MacDonald P. Jackson, and Duncan Crary among many others.

I would, of course, like to thank John Whalen of Cider Mill Press Book Publishers, who helped make this book a reality. Were it not for his excitement, enthusiasm, and faith in me, I might have given up under the weight of this massive project. I also owe a huge debt of gratitude to Mim Harrison and Cider Mill staffers Brittany Wason, Kelly Gauthier, Annalisa Sheldahl, Cindy Butler, and many others who helped mold a rather large manuscript into readable shape.

I need to add a note of thanks to my parents and extended family who always tried to make Christmas a special time. And a special thanks my sons, Dylan and Dawson, whom I have taken too much time away from in order to pursue not only this work, but also my other professional aspirations. I have tried to attend as many of their events as possible, but there is no replacement for an evening's conversation or time spent together. I owe it to them to spend more time hanging out and less time working.

Photography Credits

About Cider Mill Press
Book Publishers

Good ideas ripen with time. From seed to harvest, Cider Mill Press brings fine reading, information, and entertainment together between the covers of its creatively crafted books. Our Cider Mill bears fruit twice a year, publishing a new crop of titles each spring and fall.

"Where Good Books Are Ready for Press"

Visit us on the web at
www.cidermillpress.com
or write to us at
PO Box 454
12 Spring St.
Kennebunkport, Maine 04046